The Guinea Fowl Girl

VAL SHERWELL

THE GUINEA FOWL GIRL

A Colonial Childhood
Southern Rhodesia 1939-1958

2012

Fastnet Books
227 Donnelly Street
Armidale, New South Wales, 2350
Australia

www.fastnetbooks.net

publishing@fastnetbooks.net

© Val Sherwell 2012

All rights reserved. No part of this book may be reproduced, stored in a retrieval system, or transmitted by any form or by any means, electronic, mechanical, photocopying, recording, or otherwise, except as may be expressly permitted by the applicable copyright statutes or in writing by the Publisher.

First published 2012

National Library of Australia
Cataloguing-in-Publication entry:

Sherwell, Romola Valmai, 1939 —
The Guinea Fowl Girl: a colonial childhood Southern Rhodesia 1939-1958

ISBN-13: 978-0-9871712-7-6
ISBN-10: 0987171275

*To my children Dean and Belinda Sherwell,
a bit of family history for your interest.*

Contents

Foreword		1
PART ONE		5
Chapter 1	Que Que 1945	7
Chapter 2	The Residency	21
Chapter 3	Friendships	38
Chapter 4	Life with Our Servants and the Village School	47
Chapter 5	How Did We Amuse Ourselves?	55
Chapter 6	The Royals Come to Town, 1947, and Holiday in Fish Hoek, 1948	62
Chapter 7	Mum's Family	78
Chapter 8	'She came not but made default'	84
PART TWO		99
Chapter 9	The Convent	101
Chapter 10	Guinea Fowl	116
Chapter 11	Fort Victoria	152
Epilogue:	Que Que Again, 1956	161
Acknowledgements		169

List of Illustrations

Frontispieces
Dad (Ted Hawkey), Gran Bradbury, author and Mum (Pat Hawkey), Salisbury. c.1940
Map of Southern Rhodesia (sketched by the author)

Contents

Que Que in the 1950s	6
Mum with crepe myrtle	19
Mum, John and the 'Merk' on Remembrance Day	22
Mum, John and me in our lounge c. 1946	30
A fox terrier like Timmy	34
Mum with new hairstyle and dress	37
Maggie and Jane	44
Grandad and John, outside Lanark Hotel, c. 1948	70
Grandad and Dad, outside Lanark Hotel, c. 1948	72
Dad at Fish Hoek c. 1948	74
Grandma Bradbury and me c. 1945	79
Aunt Romola aged 21 years	80
Patricia Bradbury aged 21 years	80
Dad – John Edwards (Ted) Hawkey, at palm tree c. 1937	88
The Residency, Fort Victoria, 1999	100
Rhodes statue, Bulawayo	104
Historical Bulawayo	105
Anthony Vernon Bradshaw (Tony), while at London School of Mines	115
Guinea Fowl School Badge	121
A pair of show-offs: Riva and me, 1956	122
Guinea Fowl First Eleven Hockey	127
Guinea Fowl First Eleven Rugby	128
Guinea Fowl cadets, 1956	133
Gordon and Valmai Bradbury, wedding c. 1937	139
The Bradbury children, Howard and Jillian	140
The author aged 18	141
My cousins, the Bradbury children Howard, Jillian and Heather, c. 1953	142
My cousin Jillian Bradbury on her marriage to Rev. John Knight	143
Mrs Boggie's clock, Gwelo	144
John (second from right) and Shorty Steyn (right). Others unknown	155
Zimbabwe Ruins	157
Aunt Romola and the twins, Christopher and Adrian c. 1957	163
Mum and Tony's Wedding Day with friends, 1953	164

Dad (Ted Hawkey), Gran Bradbury, author and Mum (Pat Hawkey), Salisbury. c.1940

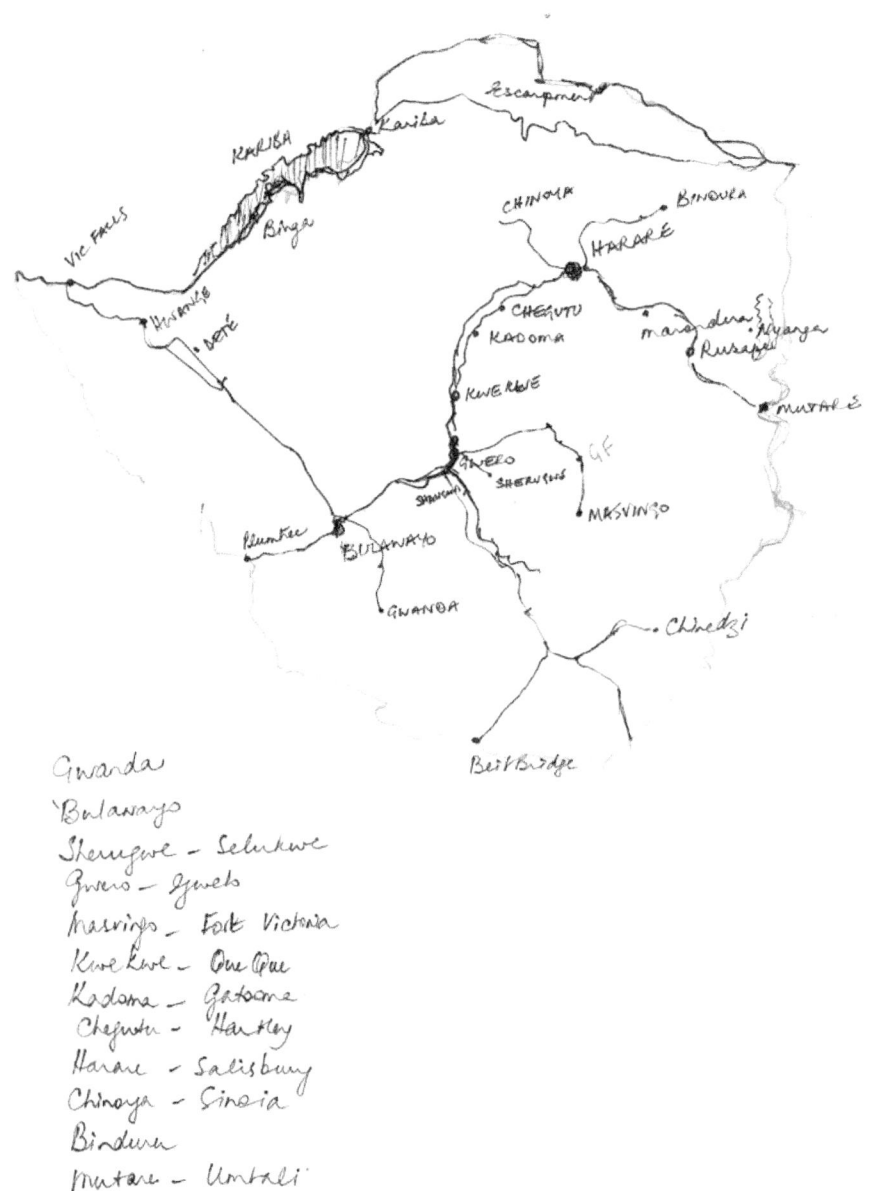

Map of Southern Rhodesia (sketched by the author)

Foreword

This account of my life starts in Que Que, Southern Rhodesia, the nucleus around which I have based most of my memoir. I have other reminiscences which have a dreamlike quality of places and times, some of when I was very young, before John, my brother was born, so probably when I was two years-old.

The first one is my father's black car. We were I believe living in Gwanda, so it must have been 1941, or thereabouts. Gwanda is a Godforsaken place today, but the magistrate's house then was like all civil servant homes in Rhodesia with an elegantly laid out garden with large trees and a wide driveway. The garden in Gwanda at the front was extremely shady because of the trees' spreading canopies, some of which flowered in spring or summer. Shade was needed because it was an extremely hot spot. I know there was a long, wide verandah but that is all. Dad's car was a little upright vehicle, a Ford. Shiny black. Our small dog had a curled up tail and was called Lucky, who, according to Mother knew when Dad was due home after work. Either he could hear the car or knew by the time of day that Daddy would return. I believe Lucky was run over one afternoon when Mum was walking with me in my pram. In a strange way I was to blame for his death, but could never understand why or how. Perhaps Lucky ran out onto the road during our walk and was killed. I remember Mother crying one night, Dad was out. Was it because he had gone to the pub, had they quarreled or was it due to the death of her dog? I know I found her tears distressing, I simply could not understand why Mother cried! I can see her dark hair, there were green curtains in the room and I remember touching her face and feeling the tears on her cheek. Next day she was her usual self.

•

'Ring a ring a rosies, pocket full of posies, hush-a-hush-a, all fall down'.

Little brown shoes, white frilly socks, full skirt all around me as I sit on the lawn. My little friends are also sitting there.

We get up, form a ring and this time we get into another circle and one of us walks around behind the children and recites: 'I wrote a letter to my love and on the way I dropped it. One of you has picked it up and put it in your pocket. It wasn't you, it wasn't you, but it was YOU'. (Meanwhile the hanky had been dropped behind someone.) The children laugh and clap and on it goes. I can't do this very well and Mum shows me how and where to drop the hanky.

Daddy plays a made-up ditty on his ukulele. He sings: 'Here comes Maeve and Robert here comes Giffy Carey', and incorporates all the names of my little friends at my birthday party. We all wear coloured hats and there are many hued balloons, pink, yellow, green, white – all trembling slightly, their string tails moving from side-to-side. There's ice-cream and cake. I have a white hanky around my head and try to pin the tail on the donkey. Mum holds my hand and guides me to the spot where she has drawn a donkey on a piece of brown paper. I pin the tail in the donkey's eye. Everyone laughs and exclaims!

The arrival of my brother from hospital – that was an occasion.

I look into the pram; a small creature is lying there. Our nanny picks him up and takes him to a change-table. I follow her. She undoes a large pin and takes off his nappy. I am shocked at the contents. Small creature is very smelly.

We have a long netted veranda, miles long. I am pushing a stool from one end, head down, I crash into the wall at the other end, cutting myself. I still have the scar under my lip. I am prone to accidents during these early years.

•

Somewhere else, the children in the neighbourhood and I are playing in the back lane where all the sanitary buckets are picked up overnight. There is a stationary lorry in the lane. It belongs to an Indian fruiterer who had just finished his delivery rounds of fruit and vegetables. We bank up behind the lorry and, unbeknown to him, we all play a pretend game and 'push' his lorry when he starts the engine and it turns over. We hang onto the bumper and back access handle and other assorted protuberances. One particular day it all goes wrong. We line up as usual; the fruiterer boards his truck. The engine starts, the lorry shoots forward in a cloud of dust, the kids sensibly fall away, but not this child. I could not and did not let go, and am bumped down the rutted lane over stones and pebbles, getting badly cut knees. The kids all shriek and the poor driver eventually stops. My mother rushes out and there is a great hullabaloo! I have scars on my knees from this incident, and I remember being in bandages for quite a time, and of course enjoying all the attention I got because of my accident.

One evening my Aunt Romola's boyfriend Ginger, in his brown army uniform with shiny buttons (it was during the war years so sometime between 1939 and 1945), drops a live fish into my bath. It is a silver fish and looks very large to me.

It is such an unusual event no child would ever forget that experience (soldier ... shiny buttons, brown uniform ... small child ... LARGE fish).

I have asked Romola about this man and she merely tosses her head and says he was totally 'unsuitable' and she could never take him seriously. ('Suitable' was the sort of word my family used, plain, utilitarian and unfussy.)

Dad, being a magistrate, moves every two or three years on the judicial circuit. By the time he and Pat (my mother) got to Que Que in 1945 they had lived in Bulawayo, Salisbury, Gatooma, and Gwanda. We move into the Que Que Hotel for a short while after we arrive at that town and have rooms on the ground floor overlooking the main street. Mum and Dad read stories to me in the evenings, and show me the comics. One of them is Curly Wee, a piglet with the curliest little tail imaginable. I in turn, read very well and read endlessly to my parents all the words of the street hoardings, the advertisements and the names and logos on buildings.

'Look Mum, Look Dad pe – he – troll, petrol'!

I am sure they found it tedious in the extreme, but I was fascinated at my ability to make sense of those symbols. It was the flowering of knowledge, but like most children I had no feeling of who I was, things just were.

It was back there – back in Que Que Southern Rhodesia, where a strange, perhaps incomprehensible childhood, and all our family troubles began; though I have no doubt that the seeds had lain dormant for a long time before the family's arrival at that town.

VAL SHERWELL

Part One

Que Que in the 1950s.

– 1 –

Que Que 1945

We moved into the Que Que Hotel, when I was nearly six years-old and my brother, John, three. I remember the hotel because of its brown bricks. The rooms the family shared opened onto a veranda with granolithic floors and a small grassy patch which ended with a silvery fence at the kerbside of the main road. This fence was about as tall as my brother. Across the road came the 'ping ping' of tennis balls. 'Good shot' someone cried, and, 'Game, game you've won'. The players wore white clothes and *takkies*[1] and some of them watched the others from the pavilion. At the far side of the twin tennis courts there were masses of dark shrubs, probably oleanders. On one side of the hotel there was a service station which had a glorious purple bougainvillea growing up and around a sturdy street light stanchion.

Several other families were accommodated along the same veranda of the Que Que Hotel, for it was a place where new residents stayed before finding a home, or alternatively having sold up lived there before leaving the town. I couldn't bear some of the people who were there. The kids stared, and their mothers, in their beige-coloured long cardigans called me 'spit-fire'; and as I yelled at any of them who spoke to me, perhaps the tag was deserved. All I wanted to do was read *Barbar the Elephant* with Mum and not be bothered with them. I don't know why I disliked them, I just didn't take to them. Maybe Mum had a bad opinion of them, perhaps she mentioned something derogatory about them to Dad, which I overheard and I was influenced in my opinions. It is quite likely I was guarding my toys from predatory children. Who knows?

Needless to say I was thrilled to leave the hotel for our brand new home.

What exactly was Que Que, apart from a small midlands town in Southern Rhodesia?

---

[1] Something like an English plimsoll.

Indigenous people had given the area the name of Kwe Kwe long before the whites came with their overlay of British colonialism, and it was so called because of the sound made by croaking frogs along the river banks. The frogs are long gone but it is 'Kwe Kwe' today. In the 19th century there were 'rumours of an *El Dorado* which attracted British fortune hunters from South Africa, and information about the gold in the region has been known for at least 1000 years'. The white inhabitants referred to it as 'QQ' and this shortened form was due to the registration plate on vehicles of people living in the town and surrounds, which was QQ. The town was small, the main road northbound to Salisbury, and south to Gwelo and like most roads in that era, once you left the town centre, the road became a stripped tarmac affair. You placed the wheels of your car on either side of two strips of tar and drove. Facilities were pretty primitive so we all accepted this form of road making.

Then, one day a yellow steamroller, a huge thing, turned up close to the edge of town as did the tar-maker. We kids watched fresh tar with its acrid smell being prepared in the rotating barrel, then mixed with gravel and laid on to the surface of the road. Perhaps they pulled the strips up first, or maybe laid the new tar in between, I don't know. But, they were building a new fully tarred road. And when it was ready we called it the 'new road'. For years afterwards it was still the 'new road' as in, 'We're going to Gwelo on the new road', and for all I know it could be the 'new road' today.

The town lay between two rivers, the Que Que River to the south and the Umniati to the north. Milestones, those white, cemetery-like slabs, pegged the distances from and to the outlying towns, and the Umniati was, in the vernacular, at the 'five mile *pig*'. (Ah! Those flat Rhodesian vowels!) The bridges crossing these rivers were built right down to the water's edge so that in times of floods, had you visited another town such as Hartley, and arrived at the bridge after the rains started, you were stranded. This was so exciting! John and I would get out of the family car, kick off our shoes and walk to the now much expanded river's edge. There were many lightning strikes, 'crack', 'crack'. We shivered in anticipation of the rolling thunder that would follow.

'Quick, quick count to five', I'd tell John.

I had been told that you should count five seconds after the lightning struck and if the thunder came immediately you could expect a downpour. But when the gap between the lightning and the thunder got larger, the storm was passing. Then, there'd be a light drizzle, the sky a pale gray/silver which added to the turbulence and atmosphere. How our parents cursed the inconvenience of being stuck on one side of the bridge. If it was hard rain we'd sit in the car, mostly with Dad because Mum did not accompany him when he was gadding about (Dad gadded a lot), watching the gray waters pounding down filled with branches and logs which crashed into one another and swept past. Occasionally an impatient driver would try and fjord the swollen river only to be washed away which resulted in a few deaths over the years. Sir Robert Tredgold relates a story in his book, *The Rhodesia That was My Life*, an accident that occurred near Umvuma which illustrates this phenomenon very well. A car with six occupants was washed over the drift of the Umzingwane River, near West Nicholson. It was raining and all the windows of the old-fashioned sedan were tightly closed. This apparently acted as a diving bell and kept the water out. However, the occupants were imprisoned and could not open or break the windows. They were saved, as it turned out, because an enterprising road overseer, noticing the incident, dispatched his African labourers down the river. He then came down on the flood, got a purchase on the car, broke the windows, and, according to Tredgold, '... the occupants were shot out in the rush of air and caught by the waiting Africans as they were swept down the river'.[2] During my early teenage I had many recurring dreams to do with furious water. I'd be walking down the road, barefooted and cold; the dull opaque, green menacing waters on either side rolling over me with a *swoosh*. The reality of our helplessness in the face of wild nature was carved into my psyche like a frightening, yet beautiful, piece of engraving.

Que Que, as mentioned earlier, was situated in the midlands, and like most midland towns the world over it was not anything you wanted to boast about. However, it had gold and minerals and good farming land. If distance is the tyranny in Australia, in Rhodesia it was geographical isolation, a small white population and the self-absorption that comes from not questioning ones' reason to be, and to that end there is no need to question why midlands towns are deemed terminally boring. The grown-ups certainly had enough parties to while away the time, and seemed content with that. We children loved it,

---

[2] Sir Robert C. Tredgold, *The Rhodesia That was My Life*. London: Allen and Unwin, 1968, pp. 41 and 42.

although young we had a sense of the freedom and naturalness of life, we wandered around the bush barefooted and fancy free. We did not notice how dusty it was or how stick-dry the winters were when not a drop of rain fell for three months.

•

Soon, we moved into our new home. There were lots of trees, eucalyptus, spathodea, euphorbia hedges, msasa and firs to name a few. Within a few weeks I was astride the branches of the largest one, my legs wound around the branch, body arched, arms and hands hanging below the level of my head. Mum came out, she looked fierce.

'Get down, you'll kill yourself. Will you get down or I'll take the brush to you'. Needless to say I didn't like the brush, so early on complied. Later, I would shin down and she would chase me, but I always ran too fast for Mum to catch me which annoyed her. There was always a clash of wills between Mum and me!

Every morning Esther, our maid, packed our tea break snacks into our little school bags. We walked to school from the back gate, across a deserted unsealed road, through a patch of bush and there we were. Though socially we were restricted by our colonial upbringing, physically we had nothing to fear. We went out to play with each other during the weekends and might be away until dark. Our parents were not preoccupied with our safety; they had no need of that. No-one ever locked a door or window of house or car. There was an incident once, years later, when someone went into our pantry and stole food. It made the local paper as this was so unusual.

However, we weren't allowed to play with 'just anybody', our parents felt their position in society and we were expected to be well mannered, always tidily dressed and work hard at school.

What I remember most about my early life in Rhodesia was the smell of oleander blooms. I would breathe slowly into their beautiful pink depths and hope I could capture the perfume and distill its essence in my head. Also, the flowering shrubs, I soon knew some of their names. The red poinsettia, the vivid orange flowers of the African tulip tree with its long yellow stamens and brown pendulous seed pods, Dutchman's Pipe which scrambled upwards in a shady nook, bougainvillea spreading. Hibiscus, bauhinia, camel's foot; somehow flowers and their perfume and Rhodesia are linked. And not only flowers, but the tall grasses with their pale pink and brown seed heads. My brother and I pulled the grasses and chewed on their tender ends. 'Sis man', the locals intoned, 'You don't know if dogs have weed on them'. We did not care about dog's wee. We loved the succulence of the fresh tips.

We lived close to town and went to its centre several times a week to swim or visit friends. Sometimes Mum took me shopping for clothing, both for herself and for me. The shops were situated in the middle of the central thorough-fare. This was a completely straight street that ran at right angles to the main Salisbury highway, traversing a steep hill at the western end. While walking up the street, Mum, in her gloves and hat, heels click-clacking all the while, nodded at acquaintances who greeted her, 'Good morning Mrs Hawkey'. The first place we passed once we had rounded the corner from the aforementioned Que Que Hotel was Paul's Fruiterers. Their shop was painted glossy green and the fruit lay on boxes, quite flat, nothing fancy. The Pauls were dark skinned with slightly greasy hair, especially Mrs Paul who wore hers long. There was something odd about them; short and squat and seemed to be there merely to dispense fruit and vegetables and give out change: they hardly spoke a word to any of their customers. We'd stand in the shop and Mum would address them. 'Good morning, I'd like some potatoes', pointing at the tray. Mr or Mrs Paul would weigh them out, seeking Mum's approval when the amount was just right. Then she pointed at something else, and that too would be weighed in a large silver sugar scoop style tray hanging from a silvery chain. Mr Paul removed a pencil from behind his ear and slowly wrote in an uneven hand the price on a piece of paper. He silently took the money, gave Mum her change and nodded pleasantly to her. Sometimes he smiled. Today I realise the Pauls probably came from the Lebanon, spoke little English and just looked out of place among all the Anglo-Saxons and Africans.

The C&A Newsagent was next. That's where you bought glue, pens, pencils mostly yellow with small brown lettering and a rubber with a silver attachment at the top. Some had rubbery figures stuck on the end – a little horse or dog or a boy or girl with soft bodies and rather hard arms and hands. They had pale features, black hair and black eyes. The boys wore pink or green shorts and the girls' white or yellow dresses. I'd push and squash them distorting their faces (nobody noticed). There were piles of newspapers, the *Que Que Observer, the Bulawayo Chronicle* and *Salisbury Herald,* coloured papers and lots of other interesting stationery. The manageress was heavily built with white hair she wore in a bun. A jolly soul as I remember. 'Hullo', she said kindly, 'How are you Borgie?' Mum said she had 'green fingers', which she explained meant she could grow anything in her garden. She told me it was because of her beautiful Michaelmas daisies, which had won prizes at the Que Que show, and that's how she gained her reputation. I wanted to see these flowers so one day walked past her house; there they were, a riot of Michaelmas daisies in pink and mauve running the length of her garden fence.

On the right hand side of the main street further up under an overhang held up by posts was McKeown the Chemist, which had wooden doors and counter. I loved its beautiful window inlaid with coloured red and green glass. It looked to me like a church window, but I could see no signs of Mary and baby Jesus and found out it was specially designed to resemble the 'apothecary bottle', which Mum said was a special bottle used by Chemists.

At this point you could see the demountable opposite, where they made milk shakes and ice-creams. Inevitably, I would say, 'Mum can I have a milk shake?' 'Please! Please, Mum'. Mostly she agreed to buy me one, rarely she refused. If she resisted I would sulk and yell a bit. Mum, who was a disciplinarian, hated adverse public attention so she'd give in and I would get my milk shake.

There was an American cartoon published in one of the national papers at that time. The characters wore a baseball cap and frequented 'drug' stores and drank 'sodas', as the Americans call them, we called them 'milkshakes' and thought they were the same thing. On offer were raspberry, caramel, vanilla and a bilious looking green concoction called lime soda.

'Well, what do you want, Borgie?' asked Mum. I dithered. 'Oh! Maybe the lime soda'. I looked at the bottles, 'No, um, um...'

'Do make up your mind. I haven't got all day'.

'OK', I breathed hard. 'The caramel then'.

The waiter put the metallic cup on the counter. I loved the cold, shiny, surface. I drew on the surface and watched the beaded droplets turn into a slow trickle running down the side of the cup and wetting the counter, while all the while slurping the frothy contents down to the last.

After the milk shake we'd continue our shopping. The road started its slow incline, past an open dusty space with a few straggly trees followed by various dress and haberdashery shops. This was where Mum mostly bought vests, socks and pants for John and me. The local park was on the right hand side with its slides and swings, tall trees but not much in the way of flowers but it was the focal point of the town. One day some friends and I were playing on the see-saw and singing 'See Saw Marjorie Daw'. I, being the tomboy I was, started pushing myself from the ground in great leaps getting more and more buoyant and over-confident, while little puffs of dust slowly filled the air. Suddenly, my side of the plank came down to the ground with a crash. I was thrown upwards from the see-saw and hurtled to the ground, landing on my back. I was winded, gasping, I thought I would die, but soon recovered my breath and equilibrium I know this has probably happened to half the kids in the world only I thought I had had a unique experience!

Opposite the park was the Que Que Post Office, a brown brick no-nonsense building. Later, as the population grew, it got too small and was rebuilt in another section of the town. This time it was a whitewashed affair, more spacious and serviceable, with its flat-sided tower, and identical clocks on all four sides. The replica of this style can be seen in so many post-British colonial towns throughout the world, and there was one in every town in Rhodesia.

I liked Crowther's General Store, which was almost at the top of the main street. It had red granolithic steps up from the street to the entrance. This seemed very grand. No other store in Que Que was so imposing. Crowther's was spacious and had wooden floors. Walking across the floors was noisy from people's footsteps and I found the creaking intriguing. Best of all I could admire the contents of the open shelving in the toy department. Mr Crowther, apart from owning the shop, was a panel beater, a tough and frightening looking man burnt dark brown, with black hair and eyes and a few tattoos, which was unusual for our community. He did not work in his store but had a manager. One afternoon late while at Crowther's, Mum was horrified to see John's busy little hands filling his school case with sweets from the shelves which were at his eye level. He was probably about four or five. I looked at Dad, expecting him to be cross, but he was laughing, and taking my cue from him, I thought it mighty funny too. Mum apologised to all and sundry. The staff chuckled, amused and forgiving. That was the effect John had on people, he was forgiven everything with his angelic smile and pudgy hands. In my childhood, John whom I loved, was also my nemesis as I felt deeply that he was 'Mummy's favourite, just because he is a boy'.

At the top of the hill where the road forked stood the Anglican Church. Pretty, it was built of stone with large shady trees and a green hedge around the perimeter. The original road carried on up to the suburbs and on the left-hand side another road entered, but on the right of the church the road took a bend up to the Globe and Phoenix Gold mine with its Club which was built in what was regarded as a salubrious area. The homes around that area were particularly pleasant with many shade trees, bougainvillea, jacarandas, bauhinia, all the shrubs for which Southern Rhodesia was once famous. Above the Club was the gold mine. We never went there, it was never stated but we knew it was out of bounds. In front of the Club the road was widened to fit in parked cars and there was a large outdoor banner advertising films for the local cinema.

Dad often went to the Club where he played snooker and drank with his cronies. Mother called these people 'bar flies' and in particular she singled out a Scot called Sandy Fraser who had red hair and was always at the Club. Mum suggested that 'bar flies have nothing in common with each other except they like to booze and thereby create a false sense of friendship'.

Some Sunday mornings, Dad would take us to the Club, without Mum, where he left us to play on the lawn out at the front. A looped chain running through the top of short metal posts set at intervals took the place of a fence, with a gap for the entrance. Lean fir trees had been planted behind the fence and at one end there was a pepper tree with fat green caterpillars which ate their way through the greenery throughout the summers. They were about as thick as a thumb, serrated or banded and hairy. Rather beautiful in retrospect, but we had no appreciation of them. We stamped on them to watch with satisfaction their yellow insides oozing. On the flag pole fluttered the British standard and a gravel path led to the entrance of the Club. At the front door there were pictures in glass-fronted boxes advertising the films currently showing at the Globe and Phoenix cinema. I remember the black and white stills of Errol Flynn with a sword (Mum called it 'buckling his swash'), and women with wide eyes and large painted lips in floaty dresses. John and I would hang about with our thick glass bottles of ginger beer that Dad brought to us occasionally from the bar. Each had a glass stopper held in place by a piece of metal. Small fingers found it difficult to remove the stopper, which came off with a tired *whoosh*, followed by a little spritzy gaseous bubble. While we guzzled our cold drinks, various people arrived with their children. We'd chat gregariously with anyone who would talk to us, patted all manner of mongrel dogs, their pink tongues lolling. They licked us all over our faces and we kissed them. Some grown-ups thought this disgusting, 'Dogs are filthy animals', they'd admonish. But we ignored them.

'Come', I said to John, 'let's cartwheel'. I was learning acrobatics at school, so proceeded to show off on the lawn. Other than that we rolled over and over, John doing some silly sort of throwing himself about, yelling and scuffling. We were probably a nuisance to everyone, but we were the magistrate's children after all, so no-one took too much notice or complained about us. We were happy. Que Que was our place and that sense of place, rather than the place itself, has never really left me.

The Club's interior was an uninteresting place for children; a large cavernous room with smaller rooms dotted with chairs and tables, where people we had never seen before, sat smoking and drinking mournfully, slowly lifting their glasses of beer to their mouths and not speaking. Other rooms lead off to the right of this space, one of which was a reading room and then the toilets. I loved the reading room. All the British tabloids and magazines made their way there. They were placed on a large table. There lay the *Daily Mail* (and maybe the *Daily Express)*, bound in yellow jackets, and containing papers with overseas news from the past few months, after which they were replaced by a later batch. There were frightening stories complete with gory pictures of Reginald John Christie from 10 Rillington Place, Notting Hill and his victims; as well as their places of interment. I was shocked to read that Christie killed people, mostly women, whom he lured to his home, gassed and strangled them then stashed them behind the walls of his house and under the floor boards, or even in his garden. In his photos he looked so ordinary, like any one's uncle, balding, bespectacled, he stood in the garden of his suburban terrace house, squinting slightly at the camera. This story provided many thrilling, chilling hours of reading. When Mum found out what I was reading she had what we called 'a pink fit'. Bad enough I had read about Christie but worse than that I had read everything about the case and, furthermore, did so every time we went to the Club. I dwelt on the accounts of Christie's crimes. In particular, I relished the story of one of Christie's tenants of the three-storey terraced house, who, on tapping a section of a wall in the kitchen at the back of the house found a spot which sounded hollow. It was a door papered over. He curiously forced the door open to find three bodies stashed in front of his eyes. This was most frightening. I became fascinated with crime stories and devoured Benjamin Bennett's books like *The Evil that Men Do,* with its gory tales, including that of the South African Daisy de Melker who poisoned three husbands and her son. This was a thrilling story, the facts went around in my head, I imagined Daisy, a fat lady by her photo, and how she bumped off her spouses and even her son. My head was full of these images.

Off the reading room was the pool room with four pool tables at the end of which was the bar, therefore this part of the Club was out of bounds to us though I saw the inner sanctum a few times. The players drank beer, they had long sticks with a point called the cue. They rubbed the cue with chalk. Then, there was the 'put' of the cue meeting balls, and the rolling sound when they went down the pool table sock. The bar was pretty busy, we were not allowed in there because we were children. However, I was not really interested after seeing the place once. Incidentally, women never played pool or snooker in Rhodesia, as this was regarded as 'not very nice' for females.

Films arrived at the bioscope (cinema) about five years later than most other places. When I was very small, about six or seven, Mum took me to see Walt Disney's *Snow White and the Seven Dwarfs*. I had many children's fairy tales at home like *Sleeping Beauty, Goldilocks, Rumplestilskin,* but this particular book worried me as I found the wicked witch a scary character. However, this was nothing compared to the terror I felt on seeing the wizened harridan on the screen. The way her long nails tried to rake Snow White's porcelain complexion. Mum was a little shocked by my reaction as she had hoped I would enjoy it. She also took me to see *The Egg and I,* which was incomprehensible to me. (I am told it was about a girl who starts a chicken farm). Later, both John and I were keen cinema goers, and although we liked Johnny Weissmuller as 'Tarzan', we especially liked Paul Guilfoyle in *Scarlet Horseman* and *Scarlet Horseman Rides Again* which was the fare at the Saturday matineés. At the time I had no idea who else starred in these serials, only that they were black-and-white westerns and the horseman wore a flowing cloak. All the kids in the village went on a Saturday morning to the bioscope, where we threw sweets, chewed gum, drank cold drinks and did the sort of things children all over the world do. There was restless anticipation, raised voices, foot stamping, squeaking cinema seats which were old, wooden framed with fraying dark green upholstery; boys punching each other, girls crying or giggling, slurping, laughing. Children ran around from seat to seat up and down the aisles, no grown up seemed to be there, ever, to quieten us and the projectionist never intervened. When the curtain was raised a hush fell upon the audience almost as if a spell had been cast. But feet were a-thrumming, and everyone whistled and yelled at the exciting parts. Each episode ended with a crisis looming for the heroic horseman, which meant we had to wait until the following Saturday – a whole week away – to 'see what happens'. At the end of the session while God Save the King, with its crackly sound, and later Queen Elizabeth (in sash and crown) was played, all the kids rose as one from their seats, and with much yelling rushed out. So much so for plebeian respect!

Also, the cinema screened popular ballet movies. And in the late forties, fifties and (I believe) early sixties a series of films came our way, some taken from Broadway musical hits. They mostly arrived a few years after they were produced in America, and I don't remember exactly when. I know we waited in anticipation for *The Music Man*, with its hit 'Seventy Six Trombones'. Gene Kelly, who played a vaudevillian, in a pink and white striped suit, with his magical tenor voice took us to the ball game in *Take Me Out to the Ball Game*, while Leslie Caron and Gene thrilled us in *An American in Paris*. But best of all, *Singin' in the Rain* was a favourite, Gene circling around and around while inundated with water. It was so romantic. I've loved movies ever since.

The cinema with its exit doors on each side doubled up as a dance hall at which time all the chairs were removed and a band set up on the stage. We young girls learnt all the dance steps, and in particular a set of steps performed in a square formation that went very well with the music of 'Lambeth Walk'. As soon as there was a break in the music we'd nag the local band, 'Play the Lambeth Walk, please, play the Lambeth Walk, paleeze'. They obliged initially, but after two such intercessions told us to go away, which we did, muttering and sulking in the corners. At the end of the evening everyone joined in the Spotlight Dance. I found this fascinating. Couples dancing, swirling around and around with a spotlight moving over them. When the music stopped, the couple who had the ill-fortune of finding the light beaming upon them would leave the floor. This continued until there was one couple left, the winners of the dance. (A grown-up form of musical chairs).

At other times the cinema was used for meetings and also provided a place for ballet lessons and rehearsals, plays and concerts. We always went to see the pantomime *Peter Pan* at Christmas. Once, the local amateur dramatic company put on *Fumed Oak*. I went with Mum and Dad, John was left sleeping at home with the maid doubling up as baby-sitter. There was the town's Dr Dewe playing a half-dressed Adjutant, (or maybe that was another play). Anyway, as far as *Fumed Oak* was concerned I could not understand it. Afterwards Mum and Dad said it was 'Too terrible, an absolute travesty, shocking acting'. But, I was puzzled because when they came across the actors and were asked how they had liked the play, they murmured in unison 'Very good, yes very good', and changed the subject.

Outside the cinema, at the front, was the monument to the fallen in the two great wars, also surrounded by a looped chain and posts sheltered by dark green fir trees, from which the ground sloped away to the park. Remembrance Day services were held there, and on those days the locals sported red poppies in their button holes or lapels.

Apart from the Que Que Hotel there was a hotel in town called Friends Hotel, it was a bit down-at-heel and was situated in a side street with rooms to let both in the hotel and over the road where there was a series of rooms which opened out onto a square. Later the Sebakwe Hotel was built at the point where the Gwelo road left the town. The Sebakwe became the place to be seen. All the town's whites patronised the Sebakwe including our parents and their friends. Mum said it had good accommodation and a bar and restaurant.

On my return visit to Zimbabwe in 1999, I walked past the Sebakwe, the reception area a filthy place with dark stains on its green inner wall. It had an enclosed brush-fenced outdoor drinking area from which emanated lots of laughter! I regret I did not go inside to suss out what the locals were doing.

At the eastern end of the town, on the flat, lay the railway station where beautiful red flowering flame trees had been planted to the north and south of the building. The station building itself was the usual whitewashed concrete edifice favoured by colonial architects. Its approaches ran from the Que Que Hotel down an unsealed road, past an open space bounded by tall trees where visiting circuses, Luna Park and other special activities were staged. On the right hand side of that road were the houses of the railway workers' families, hidden from view, their access road was dirt, unsealed and pot-holed.

Naik's Emporium, an imposing pile, was another well-known landmark.

Mr Naik, whom Mum referred to as 'Old Naik', had great sartorial elegance and sold men's suiting and clothing. His shop lay in the Indian part of town with its untarred streets. Occasionally Mum visited the shop and sometimes I went with her.

Mum with crepe myrtle

'Good morning Mrs Hawkey'. Naik would smile. His three-piece gray suit, white shirt and royal red tie a contrast to those people in the area, the Indian poor.

'What brings you here?' He had the whitest teeth imaginable, whiter than that of a mielie cob, against his smooth, chocolatey skin.

'Hullo', he greeted me. 'My you are growing up to be a big girl'.

I felt uncomfortable, hot and sticky, probably because, although I was young, from under my fringe I observed his well-manicured nails and noticed Mr Naik was very handsome. All the while I heard from the back of the shop, the whirring of sewing machines starting and thrumming as they built up speed. He employed an Indian tailor or two who busily made up orders in the back of the shop. He and Mum chatted about her needs.

Hypnotic and rather nostalgic music, which made me feel inexpressibly sad emanated from the record shop next door, where they sold *Decca* 78s. The pavements were cracked and dusty, the dusty, dusty colour that impregnates everything because it is never cleaned. Even the trees with exhausted leaves were brown, dirty, wilted, longing it seemed, for a refreshing drop of water. I watched the Indian women in their saris with the red spots on their foreheads and jewels in their noses as they slowly and graciously sauntered by. Men stood in doorways gazing into the wide, expansive sky. The little kids with their dark shiny skin and black hair stared or shyly smiled, for they were not used to whites in their streets. Then with hand to mouth ran into one of the doorways. Oh! I liked the Indian part of town, but was only allowed there if Mum took me. Something about its differences, the smells and colours got to me.

There were the usual hairdressers, Barclays and Standard Bank, dry cleaners, and service stations. We never saw the native location or dog pound. They were deemed out of bounds and we were not curious children. We heard Mum and Dad talk about the location, but to us it was just a place where we were told 'the blacks lived'. Que Que was a place of concise and neat sections, very orderly and rigid, colonial control at its most efficient, quite different from the uninhibited chaos of Kwe Kwe today.

– 2 –

The Residency

We lived in the Residency as my father was the local magistrate and Civil Commissioner.[3] In 1999 I visited two of our old homesteads and was appalled at the state of decay, for in our days the Residency in Que Que and, later, Fort Victoria were comfortable and fairly good-looking houses, not like the beautiful thatched farm houses in Kenya nor the smart homes in Salisbury, with their long driveways, dormer windows and tiled roofs and certainly nothing to match the British stately manor, but very acceptable by regional colonial standards. The Que Que home was made of boards, nicely painted and decorated and situated in a large garden which extended over an acre or more, along a dirt road on a rise away from the town and, as mentioned, close to the local school. We had three inside servants, a houseboy, cook and a coloured maid.

Every week day an African guard smartly clad in fresh khaki with puttees and a curled-brim hat, rather like the Selous Scouts, would arrive from the local gaol with about six prisoners who kept the garden under control. We loved the early morning flag raising when, shortly after the arrival of the prison gang, the guard raised the British standard on to the flagpole which was on the left-hand side of the drive, close to the entrance of the house. The unwinding of the white rope, pulleys squeaking as with a slight tremble the flag was manoeuvred to its pinnacle. We waited for the guard's salute. He did this with great ceremony, his boots crunching the gravel and his hand to his hat, palm forward. Sometimes I tried to converse with the guard, who answered in monosyllables. Sadly, I am not sure if that person, who stood patiently overseeing his charges was the same person or one of a variety, as I never looked closely at him (them).[4]

The prisoners who wore regulation prison garb with arrows back and front of their shirts washed Dad's car (a Mercury which he called 'the Merk'), raked

---

[3] Sort of District Governor.

[4] I was told in 2002 the guard was one person who was called William!

the gravel, clipped, weeded, and cleaned up the garden rubbish: meanwhile the planting and picking of flowers was done by my mother who liked her garden and had reason so to do, because it was very nice, with its bright flowers and green lawns mown to within an inch of growth. Mum cut her flowers for the vases indoors, so, most times the house was filled with a lovely perfume. Our home was kept meticulously; cleaned daily by our servants. All the furniture was moved around, the floors polished and furniture dusted, 365 days a year. Everything was in pristine condition, for the Rhodesian Civil Service, circa 1940s, was synonymous with Public Works, and I do not remember a single thing coming apart or breaking.

Mum, John and the 'Merk' on Remembrance Day

Incidentally, I never spoke to the prisoners at their dreary labours, but I knew we were held in utmost reverence. I knew this by the way we were addressed and the fact that they distanced themselves from us, averting their eyes when we approached.

A fine green hedge with a pale yellow trumpet-style flower surrounded the property, except for a small section which abutted the bush on the eastern side. I especially liked the large gnarled tree outside the house, at the front, for it had such a solid look about it. There was a fishpond at its base, around which a gravel drive snaked its way to the garage at the back. Dad seldom parked the 'Merk' in the garage, he liked it close at hand in the front drive. Why? Because he did not have to walk around the back to fetch it. Instead, he could sit on the veranda and admire it, for he was inordinately proud of this vehicle.

All the garden beds had pointed brick edges. There were two lush sections of lawn. The hedges which partitioned the front and side garden separated the fruit trees from the garden beds. This gave shape to a completely square piece of land. There were many scented flowering bushes and trees. We climbed the African tulip tree, which was on the edge of the northern lawn and from there you could see the avenue of silky oaks which formed a natural break to the cultivated part of the garden; pink oleanders, and frangipani, both yellow and pink lined the drive and the bare earth behind. Throughout the garden were hibiscuses. At the outer edge of the gravel drive opposite the front door under the overhanging Dutchman's Pipe was a short path which led to a little formal garden with flag stones and bird-bath surrounded by crimson flowering Christ Thorn. Then there were the syringas, with their delicately perfumed pink and white flowers and which has poisonous custard-coloured berries. All too soon we learned exactly how poisonous they were.

Dad had brought home a baby buck. We were absolutely thrilled with its velvety eyes and ears and spotted pale coat. It was rather wobbly on its delicate legs and was altogether adorable. It was probably found after a shooting spree. Dad built a cage out of wire netting in the lower part of our property under the syringa tree and housed the buck there. Two days later it was dead. He, or although the buck may have been a 'she', had been eating syringa berries, we knew this because the evidence was there on the ground. I cannot describe how horrific the death of that delicate little animal was to us. Today, no-one in their right mind would try and house a baby buck without knowledge of wildlife and how baby animals survive without their mothers.

In the uncultivated part of the property there were many native trees, and at the end of the garden, right next to a road was a large eucalyptus with a smooth pale gray bark which John and I, or various friends, climbed, pretending we were Tarzan or that this was Enid Blyton's *The Magic Faraway Tree* which penetrated the clouds! Naturally it was filled with all the characters from her books, and for years we took all the parts and played various roles in a never-ending story.

Across the road ran the railway line. Mostly goods trains trundled by, but in the early hours of the morning there was the occasional comforting whistle of the passenger trains which came to Que Que infrequently, probably once a week[5]. During the intervening years the eucalyptus and the Residency parted ways, a bitumen road bisecting the garden cutting off the tree from the rest. The property is now almost triangular where once it was a perfect square.

At the back of the house behind the partitioning hedge was a swing suspended from the branch of another dark gnarled tree, as well as orange trees with very sour fruit, the blossoms of which conversely had the sweetest smell, and papaws, which regularly got uprooted in the summer storms and a fowl hock in the north-west corner.

There was also a large, not to say majestic, fruit-bearing Marula tree. I had a bad reaction to the Marula for I could not resist the delicious fruit, and one year my face ballooned with urticeria. I was bed ridden for what seemed like weeks, but was probably no longer than seven days. The itching was unbearable! I stared at my face, a round ugly swollen moon reflected in the dressing table mirror, with childish disgust. Today that lovely Marula tree is no more.

Over on the southern boundary were the servants' quarters and the bucket-style lavatory which was emptied by the night soil 'boy' (an untouchable in African society known as the 'shateen boy'), as the house was not sewered. A garage and the rainwater tanks completed the picture.

John and I greedily ate green mangoes with their unformed pips from the heavily laden trees, the fruit of which never had a chance to ripen. There were guavas, their fruit a pinky-buff hue with rather rough edible pips. Sometimes

---

[5] Sir Alfred Beit and Cecil Rhodes were instrumental in building this Rhodesian rail, a part of the ambitious project of a railway from Cape to Cairo, and like all railways around the world opened up the country to trade and development.

Campbell, our cook, grilled them for us on the brick and iron 'braai'[6] outside the kitchen. The smoky smell imbued the fruit with delicious properties. We never thought much about the fruit and took its availability and abundance for granted.

Another section of garden was separated by the ubiquitous hedges with a second swing attached to a very large tree, in a sort of arbor, with an ungrassed section. In that space we used to play hospitals and Doctors and Nurses with lots of white sheeting for bandages. We loved having our legs and arms entwined in bandages. Mum even made me a nurse's cap with a red cross. I felt very important.

We had a highly polished red granolithic front veranda with mosquito proofing and green striped blinds from where I could see the convulvus and portulaca growing in a narrow bed outside the veranda. At one end were our living quarters, and at the other, an entrance into the lounge which was decorated very stylishly in the fashion of the day. Richly woven Chinese carpets with floral borders lay on polished floors, and a brass tray with intricate tracing attached to black wrought-iron legs was placed in one corner. It was used as a drinks tray.

Each evening, Mum or Dad called Richard, our houseboy, for nothing was done without our servants. 'Richard, please bring the drinks'. For this ritual Richard would have changed into a white uniform, for waiting at table. He'd bring whisky and brandy mostly, because no-one drank wine then. There were the cut-glass decanters and expensive glasses and a silver ice bucket with tongs. All of these were placed upon a brass tray. The tray made a particular metallic sound if anything was placed upon it or dropped upon it. It was a source of great fascination. The top shone with a warm brassy colour. If you gazed into it your deformed reflection gazed back. Moving your head caused the reflection to ripple and break. I spent many hours trying for a perfect image, but because of the way it was forged, never could.

On the mantel, close to the tray, there were many porcelain figurines and a curious wooden clock shaped like a dog. His body was made of wood and the dog's round, white saucer-shaped eyes with black pupils showed the time, one eye replacing the traditional hour hand, the other the minutes. They rotated, one quickly, the other slowly. I sometimes sat looking at the clock waiting until

---

[6] BBQ.

it was, for example, a quarter to three. A creepy feeling came over me! The dog is still in existence sixty years later, its mechanism long having given up the ghost, as it is not repairable. Finally, in our lounge was a green lounge suite, a columned standard lamp and fireplace. There is a photo taken in the lounge of the three of us. Mum, half turned towards John, a loving smile on her face and John beaming at the camera, with a happy, enthusiastic expression, while I, tousle haired, glower. You can tell a lot about family relationships from photographs.

Mum, John and me in our lounge c. 1946

Dad bought the latest radio and record player which he installed so he could play his favourite records. The strains of The Ink Spots singing 'Bless You for Being an Angel', with the heroic tenor's voice rising high, and 'Whispering Grass'. Anything by Bing Crosby, and he particularly liked Dvorak's *Humoresque* and Gershwin's *Rhapsody in Blue*. The latter he played over and over. This style of modern classical music was all the rage. The radio had metal bands over the amplifier. One day I deliberately scratched some words into one of these silver coloured bands. The silver flaked away awkwardly, leaving a nasty scar. The reason I did this? I do not know, but Dad was furious at my desecration.

'Borgie what gets into you? You are so destructive'. As Dad never laid a finger on me, his anger bit deeply. Every time I walked by Dad's radio/record player the mess I had made of the shiny bands filled me with guilt.

Finally, what stands out most significantly from our Que Que home was my mother's Chinese wall hanging of white storks, all in silk. It was a tactile pleasure to run my fingers over its silky threads, examining the yellow beaks and the slightly raised feathers. Where she got it I do not know, probably in South Africa before she married my father. We have it still, and although it is rather decrepit, it is still beautiful.

When we were young, John and I ate at a children's dining set, a yellow table and two small chairs which lived in one of the bedrooms. Esther would bring our meals to us on a tray with Bunnikins crockery and oversaw us to make sure we ate everything and not fling our food about. Later, when we grew up a bit we were allowed to eat in the proper dining room which was separated from the lounge by an arch-way. It was a sunny, spacious room as the room had windows in two of the walls. Mum had a large wooden sideboard with matching dining room table and chairs.

A passageway snaked around the house and all the bedrooms led from it. 'A complete waste of space', Mum said. Lastly, a single bathroom with a large old-fashioned bath was on the western side of the house and a kitchen with a black wood stove, scullery, and pantry. For me the telephone which was at the end of the passageway affixed to the wall was the highlight of our house. After dialing the number you had to press a bar in the handset along the middle before you could be heard by the other party. I was greatly attracted to the phone and drove Mum and Dad mad because, especially when I was about 11 years-old, I spent as much time as I could get away with, talking to my friends.

'You have just left that child, not five minutes', Mum would lecture me, 'What do you have to say to one another?' Mum did not understand there were things of vital importance to speak about! I also wondered why Mum did not understand my need to be in contact with my friends as often as possible. In fact, for an era of dropping in to see friends and neighbours whenever the mood arose, few children ever came to our home uninvited. Mum liked things to be organised and did not care for impromptu visits.

Mother tastefully decorated the main bedroom, which she shared with Dad. We were not allowed into either the lounge or bedroom without her presence or permission. She had an uncanny knack of knowing if we were in the lounge. 'Come out of there', she would cry imperiously.

Truth was I loved going into Mum's bedroom, I can see it now. I'd open the drawers in her gray dressing table and open her jewellery box. I'd lie on the bed with the box and pick through her jewellery. There were ceramic rosebud brooches, the buds the palest pink, fashioned in the image of the small pink roses growing around the town. Then I'd run my fingers through the topaz-coloured beads, each with a translucent orange beauty; her pearl necklace and earrings the milky sheen so smooth to the touch, and several silver bangles that tinkled on Mum's arms.

There were little ornaments, a porcelain creamy-coloured house with blue roof and a dab of blue for the front door and black windows. A milkmaid standing at a funny angle, her milk pail held in front of her, up high. Her dress seemed to blow in an unseen breeze. Mum had other pretty but impractical ornaments, like a Scottish terrier on a lead and a black cat, head to one side.

When and if Mum caught me in her bedroom there was hell to pay!

•

John and I had separate bedrooms with individual mosquito netting hanging from hooks in the ceilings of each room. One day, in an effort to make me more tidy, Mother came in with some flouncy material.

'Do you like this, Borgs?' she asked.

'Yes', I said, but did not care one way or the other.

'Well I am going to make you a *Dolly Varden* suite for the bedroom'.

She set to, cutting and folding, machining and pinning and completely redecorated my room with a green-frilled, kidney-shaped *Dolly Varden* dressing table and matching curtains and bed cover. They looked wonderfully fresh but I was not really interested in girlie things. So much so that my Uncle Gordon who spied me down town one day rang up my mother saying:

'Pat, I've just seen your daughter, she looks just like a 'charity child', no shoes, hair uncombed and a large tear in her dress'.

I was a tomboy it's true and untidy in my dress. I loved going without shoes. I have a photo of my brother and me, barefooted, standing next to the flagpole. I am wearing a spotted dress and a large brimmed hat. On the back is written in pencil 'John and Romola Valmai 1945'. Bush kids if ever there were, we look as if we had not a care in the world!

Mum was annoyed, most annoyed, furious in fact, probably mostly out of fright for our safety during a time when my brother and I jumped from the ledge on top of the built-in cupboards, as there was a space between those cupboards and the ceilings, onto our beds. I was scared stiff that I might fall, but I was also very stimulated. Of course, as night follows day we were thereafter in Mother's bad books. And that gave her an idea of how she would punish us.

One morning not long after the jumping incident, I noticed Mum putting up a large piece of white paper on my bedroom wall. This paper was divided into days and weeks. She had an envelope in her hand.

'What's in there, Mum'? I asked. 'You'll see', she answered mysteriously.

Once she had the paper in place she opened the envelope. There lay shiny silver and gold paper stars.

'If you and John are naughty, I am going to give you a black mark each, and...' She paused. I noticed her hair was rolled around her head in a sausage roll and was so interested in this new fashioning of her locks that I began to lose interest in these so called 'Black marks'. Then she continued, '...a gold star for really good behaviour and a silver one if you are reasonably good'.

John and I stared at her uncomprehending. Oh! We understood the words alright, but not the import of how these black marks and stars would control us, particularly as we fought so much.

One such episode is imprinted indelibly in my mind. Mum set out the Meccano set on a blanket on the veranda. I see the green striped blinds and the coloured Meccano set to this day. We siblings were making things, cars, factories, houses, limbs for people, when suddenly for a reason I no longer recall, a fight broke out between us. I bashed John with my half-made factory and he in turn laid in to me with his Meccano toy. Screams, yells, bruises and a sort of vicious need on my behalf to really hurt, not only physically. (I can only assume that my frustrations at being the child who felt unaccepted by my mother and always on the outer boiled over). It was clear that things had gone wrong, insofar as the 'black marks' were concerned and indeed we both got black marks for the Meccano incident.

'Borgs keeps running away from me', said a doleful John the very next day, his little boy's face streaked with tears.

'I don't'.

'You do'.

'Well you keep whining and crying'.

Thwack! Slap across the back of the knees, and a charcoal black mark was promptly put up against my name.

'You are not to leave your brother behind, you naughty girl. I am giving you a black mark!'

Black marks reduced us to shrieks of torment and anger. John got mostly silver and gold stars. I do not remember ever getting a star, but had black marks aplenty and never, like Peter Rabbit, understood why I could not 'now and again be good'. After a few months Mum took down the board and packed it away. Obviously the desired effect of improving my behaviour had not been achieved, and she gave up in frustration. I'd go to my room during this phase, lie on the bed and sob. Mum did not love me; that was clear. I imagined dying – that would make her and Dad regret all she'd done to me. Then I'd think about, maybe, not dying, just getting some horrid disease. They'd have to visit me in hospital. Mum would be contrite – I'd drift off, my imagination afire.

Dad often laughed about our torment over the black marks. 'John so good and Borgs so naughty'. At the end of the black marks phase when we were quite a bit older, Mum reverted to her trusty hairbrush, but as usual could never catch me.

When John was small he used to rock himself in his sleep. His rocking was so vigorous that his bed would start in one place and end up somewhere else by morning. He'd 'hurrumph!' gently to himself and the bed would slide quietly across the wooden parquet floor. He had this curious habit for many years, it worried Mum I know, and then, one day he outgrew it, just like that.

On a hot summer's day (and the Rhodesian sun could be fierce), John got sun-burned from playing outside without his hat. He was bright red all over, his face puffy, he was crying with the pain. Then he became feverish. Dr Hirsh was called. I could hear the urgency in Mum's voice.

'Maurice, come quickly, it's John'. Within minutes the front screen door opened and in came Dr Hirsh, a stethoscope hanging from his neck and falling over his tweedy-brown suit, his dark hair slicked back – that was how men wore their hair then. He and Mum and Dad whispered together. He examined John. Things were bad. For days he was not expected to live. I have a vivid picture of the doctor standing over John in one of the bedrooms, dimly lit, the soft light falling in a circle onto the carpet; there was an atmosphere of fear, people whispered and tiptoed around the house. The African servants looked grave, a sick child is a disastrous affair to Africans. But one morning, luckily, about a week later, the fever from his acute sun-stroke lifted and he got better.

Our parents were quite friendly with other magistrates in the district, not that they saw each other much. As far as the Rails from Gatooma were concerned, we visited them one weekend: they too had a large garden with palm trees. Mr Rail told us about the time he was in Egypt and watched Egyptians lying asleep under palm trees and just rolling over when the sun moved, without waking, so that they could chase the shade. They had a large Grandfather clock in their hallway, very imposing with a silver face and pendulum. It has some sort of chasing on the face and had a satisfactory boom when striking the hour.

On one occasion we were eating lunch with a young school friend of John's, whose name was Warwick Rail. (Same Rail – his father the Magistrate of Gatooma). We were seated at the little yellow table and chairs and using the Bunnikins crockery. We were probably mucking about. Suddenly, a quarrel broke out and Warwick rammed the prongs of his fork into John's cheek. They both screamed blue-murder. The house was in chaos, our maid, Esther ran around yelling for Mum. The doctor was called. John was treated on the spot. I do not know if the child concerned was sent home, or how he got there, but our parents vowed that the visitor Warwick would never be invited to our home again. And indeed that was the end of the acquaintance.

Another time poor little John visited a friend in the suburbs who had a monkey. It was a dear little chattering thing, but not a suitable pet for a child. Anyway, with or without provocation, this little creature bit John in the cheek. Here again there was outrage and fear. He survived, although I believe everyone was worried he might get some nasty disease. He was a bit prone to accidents when young.

•

Medicine in the late '40s and '50s was primitive by today's standards. If John or I had a cold, Friar's Balsam was used to unclog our chests. Every evening after our baths and dressed in our striped pyjamas, Esther would bring in a steaming white enamel basin which contained the balsam concoction diluted in water. This basin was covered by a towel to 'Keep the fumes inside where they can do good!' We hung our heads over the bowl and were covered by the towel, while Mum exhorted us to 'breathe in'. The pungent smell and acrid fumes, especially in the first five minutes or so, caught my nose and throat, there was an unpleasant burning sensation. But the boiling fumes worked their efficacious magic. Boils were drawn with an ointment and plaster. We had no side effects, but it seemed to take an age to get better. No-one, however, could find a cure for my idiosyncrasy which was sucking my index and middle fingers on the right hand. Mum tried everything, even bitter aloe, to break the habit, all to no avail. I just stopped the sucking when I was about 12 years-old.

A received 'truth' in the late 1940s was that children should have a bowel movement every day. Mum insisted that John and I sit on our enamel potties after lunch and produce a 'job'. What agony! John, being of methodical bent always complied. I was a terrible failure.

'Haven't you gone yet, Borgs?' Her voice filled with irritation.

'No, and I am bored'. This said sulkily in a tear-filled voice.

'Well stay there until you've done a job'.

'Why?'

'It will make you regular when you are grown up'.

After sitting for eternity I got off the potty with a round red ring on my bottom which itched. I hated the whole procedure and this became such an obsession that I could never comply. In the end this requirement for a healthy, regular life disappeared as new ideas about the workings of human anatomy became vogue and sitting on the potty was not one of them.

On three occasions I spent time at the Que Que Hospital, once for round worms, then to have my appendix removed and finally the guillotining of my tonsils, that is, only the heads of the tonsils were removed. For some reason, going to hospital caused me great humiliation. When spoken to I turned my face to the wall and would not answer. After a day or two I felt a little more sociable.

'Ah! You're a changed person from the little girl who came in on Saturday, (or Monday or whatever day it was)', said the assorted nurses and some of the elderly patients. And indeed, I was. I would sit up, chatter away and it was on one of these times that a woman in the bed opposite me gave me a recipe for chocolate fudge (or was it toffee?) I can still see her hands moving as she explained how to do this. The mysteries of making fudge/toffee is totally scrambled with the passage of time but it was something along the lines of 'One block of black chocolate, melt with some sugar and milk. Boil slowly until it makes a soft ball'. And so on. The end result was that hospital wasn't so bad, but the fudge/toffee never worked out, and no wonder!

Like other countries in the world, Rhodesia was swept with a polio scare. I remember Mother sitting us down and telling us all about the dreaded scourge.

'You mustn't overtire yourselves. Lots of children are getting polio', she explained. Truly she looked worried.

There was a lot of publicity about polio, and how it made you lame, or maybe you would be left without mobility in an endless paralysis. Indeed our family knew the Robertsons, an elderly couple whose lone child, Jeannie, contracted the disease. Jeannie was decidedly lame, her bad leg much enlarged, she used to walk with the aid of a stick. We sensed that everyone felt completely impotent in the face of the polio pandemic. We had to rest, not overdo any activity and our parents were told to check for temperatures. Mum also worried we might get typhoid or diphtheria. We had all the vaccinations and needles against measles, chicken pox, rubella, typhoid, diphtheria and for all I know a dozen more dreaded diseases. During that time there was talk of black-water fever, malaria and bilharzia, a nasty fluke which penetrated the host's skin. As the latter was a problem in the country, we were never allowed to paddle or swim in still waters, the home of bilharzia. Most of these scourges, apart from bilharzia and malaria have been dealt with and it is now HIV/AIDS that plagues Africa.

Mum had a love of Persian cats and we always had one or two, wonderfully fluffy they were, I used to watch them sitting in the sun, the rays picking out the fine edges of their fur. They delicately licked themselves all over, but as is well documented, this breed is not very friendly so we children never really warmed to them. However, it was around this time that a dog came to our front door wagging his little tail, the friendliest little creature imaginable. He was a black-and-white fox terrier. No-one knew who owned this little fellow, but I was enchanted with him. As was John. Mum told the neighbours about the stray, but no-one seemed to have any idea whose dog he was.

'We'll call him Timmy'.

A fox terrier like Timmy

    I do not know who decided this but the name suited him very well. We took him everywhere. He was the cutest dog, lively, bright eyed and loyal. After about 6 months we were walking with Timmy in town when an elderly woman, dressed in black, with a black hat and very white hair espied us.

    'Blighter, Blighter', she called. Timmy started barking and jumping for joy.

    'Where did you children find my Blighter?' she asked.

    'He just turned up at the front door', I said, I was after all the older of the two children.

    'Well, he's our dog you know. We lost him one weekend and always wondered what had happened to him. What are your names and where do you live?'

We told her.

'Well', she said, patting 'Blighter', 'I will visit your parents this weekend, because we want our dog back'. She was very sweet about the whole matter.

We rushed home, Timmy at our heels blithely unaware that he would soon be leaving us.

'Mum, Mum, this dog's called 'Blighter' and belongs to an old lady', I told her. Mum listened.

'What's her name?'

'Dunno'. We shook our heads, 'But we don't want her to take Timmy'.

Mother must have received a telephone call because she told us the next day that the woman's name was Mrs Schofield and she lived on a property with her husband, Old Mr Schofield. In due course Mrs Schofield arrived and took the little fox terrier away. We could see his head through their car's back window, ears pricked, as the Schofields drove out of our front gate. I felt so miserable and John cried when he left. And that we thought was the end of the matter. However, after a few weeks Mrs Schofield arrived at our front door, with Timmy/Blighter in tow.

'You had better keep the dog', she said to my mother, 'He is pining for the children'.

We were delighted, absolutely thunderstruck with joy. And so Timmy came to live with us. John thought he was his dog and I thought he was mine. It was after we moved to Fort Victoria that Timmy died while I was at boarding school at Guinea Fowl. I was busy being a teenager and did not give the dog much thought over that time, and as for John, I never asked what happened to the dog, or how John felt. Dad was so peculiar at that stage and I always wondered if Timmy was starved, left as he was a great deal of the time to the care of the African cook, or whether he died of old age, I will never know. Dad said he lay down in front of the fish pond and never woke up. Vale Timmy, he was a dear little fellow who accompanied us everywhere during our early youth.

Mother liked an afternoon nap. She would lie on her bed, always with a library book, she liked biographies, but was too mean to buy books so she got them from the local library. Despite the fact Mum never bought any books, in our house there were always an assortment of reading matter, mostly bought by Dad. He had his glossies about photography and lots of books about crime and some on history. There were no women's magazines in the house, although Mum admitted she read them at the hairdresser and doctor's consulting room.

Once Mum read a book about Wallis Simpson and the King of England, who Mum told us had 'abdicated'. The story seemed to enrage her and she wandered about muttering, 'That woman, dreadful piece of work'. The woman was always to blame according to Mum who was no feminist.

She would get absolutely furious if we woke her in the afternoon, and of course, although we had acres in which to play, we always ended up playing close to her bedroom in the garden invariably waking Mum up. She was in a sour mood after that.

Mum used to paint her nails in those days, a sort of purply red, and wore a matching purply red lipstick. She was good-looking with a slim figure which she retained until she died in 2008. All the women in the '40s and '50s were keen on fashion. The new look – long-length skirt, post-World War11 was the rage; this followed by skirts with a peplum, padded shoulders and hair coiled on top of the head. Mum made most of her clothes (and mine), and was always dressed in the latest, though it must be said that 'fashion' per se, came to Rhodesia at least 18 months after Paris or Rome – the northern hemisphere season six months before was a reason, albeit only partly. She had a dress maker's dummy of her torso, every needlewoman had one. I thought it was horrible, It lurked inert on a stand, an obscene female body with no legs, hands, neck or head, made of some kind of Plaster of Paris. She had drawers full of pins, tailor's chalk, tape, scissors, tacking thread, needles, press studs, hooks and eyes, Vogue and Milady patterns. She showed me how to lay the fragile tracing paper pattern on the material.

'Be careful, allow extra material to match the pattern of the cloth', she always intoned. Then, Mum would pin everything in place, cut the notches and tack the darts.

'The notches you match to other pieces of matching notches in the pattern', she went on. Then she would carefully cut the material. Mum knew about blind hemming, bound buttonholes, clothes cut on the cross and how to blanket stitch, She was a very good needlewoman and made her clothes on her black Singer.

'An antique you know', she'd say and so it was, for it belonged to my grandmother, her mother Agnes before her.

Strangely, despite her talent she would never admit that she made her and my clothes, and I wonder if it was because it reminded her of her childhood and that her machine was the very one that Agnes used to keep body and soul together. Mum was secretive, probably the most secretive person I have met. She never mentioned her past.

Mum with new hairstyle and dress

– 3 –

Friendships

Mum was very particular about her friendships. Our parents mixed with the headmaster of the school, the manager of the Roasting Plant and his wife, the manager of Barclays Bank and his wife, dentists and local doctors, all were worthy recipients of her company. She never socialised with the teachers. The shop keepers and butchers she regarded as *infradig;* and as for motor mechanics or 'reps' (sales representatives), they were beyond the pale. In fact she thought anyone who used the word 'sales rep' instead of the proper noun was well beyond the proverbial pale. It was really very funny, especially in retrospect. John and I used to take Mum off in the manner in which she told us about whom she had regard for. I often wondered why she told us all these things. I now believe, she thought she ought to instill some sense of discrimination in us. She felt much the same about the children we fraternized with. Of course being children, we took no notice of her expressed wishes in this regard.

Firstly, there was the Tarr family, with their two children, Priscilla and Ivan who were railway people. Their modest home overlooked the flamboyant trees that lined the station precinct, giving the place a leafy and colourful feel. These children were our great friends even though Mother did not think much of them. Ivan was a small, wiry, boy, one would describe him today as being 'vertically challenged' for he was very short, and spent his spare time diving from the high-diving board at the local pool. He would bound up the steps from the pool, scale the diving board and without so much as 30 seconds for a breath, would plunge into the water and repeat the whole process. Quite a feat for such a little lad. On the other hand, Priscilla was a knowing little soul.

One summer's day while we were eating the ripe purple figs in their garden, she said,

'My Dad likes my Mum because she has big bazookas'.

'Bazookas, what are bazookas?' I asked.

She said, 'Oh! Don't you know about bazookas or titties?' she gesticulated, her little hands making curvy shapes in the air. Then she began to laugh enjoying my astonishment, and indeed I was astonished.

'All men are like that, Mum told me'.

'Like what?'

'They like ladies with big bazookas. My Dad likes big bazookas and I bet your Dad does too'. She cupped her hands to her skinny chest which she thrust out, pushing her bottom out and wiggled it around a bit.

I was shocked, I did not believe her. I asked Mum about it, but she changed the subject, which she normally did when matters of this sort arose. She did not approve. I could see by the expression in her eyes. There were other aspects of the Tarr family she did not like. Mr Tarr was a drinking buddy of my father's.

'Your father always takes up with people like that silly Old Tarr, another of his barfly friends – quite beneath him', said my mother. 'I'd prefer it if you didn't visit those people'. But we did.

I also adored Julie Theron who lived with her Afrikaans family in the *Pisé de térre* in a poorer part of town. She was blond, skinny with blue eyes and freckles and became my best friend. Mum took a particular dislike to Julie, she did not like her style, or her family, but never stopped me from seeing her.

'She is just using you', she said. But I was in love and did not understand what she meant.

When Julie and I were at the age of about 10 years-old I used to visit her for the day and we read *True Romance* magazines, with their illustrations of beautiful girls with large tear drops falling elegantly down their flawless faces. Their tragic love affairs with impossibly handsome men impressed both of us as well. We devoured *Stage and Cinema* with pictures of Gene Tierney, Pier Angeli, Lana Turner, Gregory Peck, Howard Keel etc. Placing their pictures in exercise books, interleaved with tracing paper, we gazed at them through the tracing paper which gave their faces an opalescent look. They stared out at us in all their magnificence! We sighed. 'She's so beautiful', and lightly ran our hands over the paper which emphasised their blue, green or brown eyes, pink cheeks, blond or brunette hair. As for the men, they were too dishy for words!

And so, we dreamt of love and beauty, powerful emotions stirred.

There was no salacious gossip or interest in the private lives of stars, which no-one knew anything about. They were on a pedestal with a plinth marked 'Golden and Pure', and there they remained. Everything that came out of Hollywood in that era was fairy floss and we lapped it up.

Not everything went well between Julie and me, if something happened that upset her, she screwed up her little face into a white demonic mask out of which two dagger-like eyes seemed to protrude while a stream of cruel, biting remarks emanated from her tight-lips. She often made me cry and I was terrified of getting on the wrong side of Julie, but often did.

Mum allowed me to visit Joyce Watt whose family was one of two sets of Watts. She was a tall lanky girl and also became my best friend. I don't know if she was my 'best friend' before or after or in tandem with my friendship with Julie, but it was an entirely different relationship. Both Watt families lived near the hospital and occupied two separate, but adjoining properties. One brother was wealthy and lived in a fine house while Joyce was the daughter of the family who were not as well off, and therefore their home was less substantial. The wealthy Watts were childless. Fruit trees aplenty, mostly oranges, *naartjies*[7] and grape fruit set in about an acre of garden separated the two families. They were Scottish people. Mr and Mrs Watt No. 2 had retained strong Scottish accents with their rolling 'rrrrs' which fascinated me. She had a brother, much older than she, who worked as a fitter and turner. He came to the dinner table in his vest. I knew instinctively that no-one in my family would dream of just a vest at dinner and lunch (or breakfast for that matter).

Joyce and I spent hours reading all the *Beano* comics and *Asterix*, and the large *Bumper* annuals, which were very popular at the end of the 1940s and beginning of the 1950s. My memory of this friendship is all about reading, and I always associate Joyce and the Watts with those *Girls and Boys Bumper Annuals* and especially those stories with Scots characters and accents. It was at that time I came across the word 'Omnibus', which referred to a very large annual sold at Christmas. 'Om-nee-bus'. I rolled the word around in my mouth, I wanted one of those ohm-nee-buses so badly. We occasionally went to the wealthy Watts – Joyce's uncle and aunt – and swam in their pool, but never went into the sage green tin-roofed house. They had an abundant

---

[7] Afrikaans name for mandarines and used throughout Southern Africa.

Golden Shower which always was in full flower in a mature, riotous garden.

The Reynolds who lived on a farm about five miles out of town seemed to pass Mother's scrutiny and I was therefore allowed to visit their daughter Julienne as well – another 'best friend'. They had fields of lucerne. I remember these being the greenest vegetable, almost emerald in hue, I had ever seen. 'For the cattle', I was informed. The Reynolds had a reservoir and on the first morning of any visit Julienne would say, 'Let's swim'. Feigning nonchalance I grabbed my costume, pretending to be excited and quickly changed, the cool air causing goose-bumps on pale, freckled skin.

'Jump!' Julienne would yell as she dropped from the side. The water was black and slimy and the corrugated tin sides were green with the self-same slime. I always feared swimming in its dank recesses, perhaps dragons lurked there or maybe horror-upon-horror, *snakes,* but did not let a soul know of my trepidation. However, after the first few minutes, when I realised nothing would harm me, I really enjoyed these plunges, all fear receding as we ducked and dived; splashing and choking and coughing, we'd lift ourselves up on to the sides, and using our elbows wriggle out again all ashiver!

The Reynolds' farm house was bordered with hedges of *euphorbia,* with its geometric orientation, the twigs of which broke off, snapping like chalk and oozing white milk which caused our fingers to stick together, not a nice sensation. Also, the milk could blind a person. Mrs Reynolds told us all this and said we should not play with euphorbia. If anything this made euphorbia, which was a strange green quite different from the emerald Lucerne, more fascinating and we snapped the twigs and got milk on our fingers. 'Sis', I tried to rub the stickiness off on my dress, it never really worked. We also got mulberry stains on our fingers as they had several large fruit bearing mulberry trees. 'Just pick the green ones', said Julienne, 'and rub them over the stains'. I did – miraculously they disappeared.

The Reynolds had a coat stand just inside the front door, I had never seen one before. Their farm house always smelt of seed and sacking from the upstairs attic where bags were stored. I do not know what type of seed, I only remember that there was something quite different about the Reynolds' place from our own home. Then there were the smells, sounds, wooden floor boards and large windows open to the outside. Life here was altogether a freer existence. Mrs Reynolds was not fussy about time, and noise just washed off her. We could meander around the garden at will. Sometimes, Mr Reynolds would take us for a ride on his red tractor. We ranged their farmland, it was cool on that tractor, with a slight wind and very calming. It was here that I first began to love the stories of Enid Blyton and Julianne and I would read all the *Famous Five* stories and the others, like *The Magic Faraway Tree*, which fired our imaginations. Sometimes we rode bicycles along the dirt road which led from the farm to the main road, and across an uncultivated piece of land, rocky and difficult, to the gold mine dumps on the other side of Que Que town, to the back of the public school. I spent many a happy weekend there, but like many childhood friendships we drifted apart and I do not know what has happened to her or my other friends from those days.

•

Probably the most important couple in my parents' social life were the Hossells, Frank and Maggie. We always referred to them as 'the Hossells'. They lived at a place called Rocky Ridge on the Hillandale Road, outside of the town. Its entrance was a sandstone arch, rather imposing, then, a circular drive which led to a low bungalow style house with a shiny red granolithic concrete front step and a green painted front door.

To us it was a magical place. They had about five acres with a ranging kopjie in the background; the garden was always filled with splendid flowers and fruit trees. There were stone steps and small pools. Exciting vistas opened when you walked through the garden. But the greatest fun in visiting the Hossells was they had a swimming pool in the back garden which had vibrant red Cannas growing around it. Their stone changing room was more than just that. There was a covered veranda with a roughly cast slate-tiled floor upon which the adults sat on chairs and seemed to drink for hours while the assorted visiting children played in the pool. Not many families had a pool in those days, and we called them swimming baths then. I had learned to do cartwheels and remember the control I had over my body. I cartwheeled all over the grassy surround, showing off. Then I entertained everyone to a demonstration of back-bends and splits. The grown-ups oohed! and aahed! Elixir to a child!

One Sunday I secretly entered the whitewashed house while the grown-ups were swimming, tiptoeing into the kitchen through to the pantry. I stole food. You can be sure it was something sweet. I know that I always had a desire to stuff my face with food when I was a young girl but the sense of guilt over this incident was such that I blurted out my sinful behaviour to Mum, who was not amused.

'What were you doing in the house in the first place without one of the grown-ups present? Secondly, how could you steal food from the Hossells who have been so good to all of us and whose friendship is so appreciated?'

I felt very guilty.

The Hossells had a son called Joey who was slightly retarded, a red haired fellow whom we teased rather a lot. Mrs Hossell – Maggie – was beautiful, she exuded a strong sexuality, of which as a child I was only dimly aware. She had a magnificent body of the Marilyn Monroe style, blonde hair which she wore in a long Page-boy. Her full lips (without the benefit of collagen) before such fullness was fashionable and therefore more noticeable, she emphasised with bright red lipstick. She wore strappy floral sun-dresses which suited her to perfection. Maggie was easy-going she laughed a great deal, a lovely warm womanly guffaw, loved a drink and a good time. The whole set orbited around Maggie and Pat, my mother, who was dark and small and good-looking in an entirely different way. Mum was known locally as 'the lady with the pale pink voice' and as suggested, her voice was very soft, which can be irritating when sitting in a crowded café while she mumbles away. Mum was a journalist for the town newspaper the *Que Que Chronicle*, and wrote articles of local interest which were always innovative, for she had a natural bent for writing – the letters she wrote to me were always unusual. She had the facility of finding something of value in the most ordinary everyday events. She was more intelligent than Maggie. They were best friends and made an interesting contrast! Even though I was a child at the time, I knew all the men in our little coterie fancied Maggie, although I would not have put it in those terms, (knowing nothing of gender and sexual politics), and who could blame them, she was alluring. Like many women of her era she needed and thrived on men's approval and her carefree manner and looks meant she had male admiration aplenty. She seemed very cool, untouched by poverty, insecurity and the world's woes. Years later Maggie came to live in Australia and visited Mum. Gone were the fresh, startling looks. She still had her flippant, girlish carefree laughs and made racist jokes. The world has moved on but I tend to think she has not. I still have a deep affection for Maggie, she filled so much of my early life and was very kind to all the children she knew.

Maggie and Jane

Maggie's husband was Frank – a dentist. He was the person who pulled out all my back teeth, that was what they did in those days. I found him repulsive because he had a little black moustache and looked very Welsh and snuffled when he spoke. He was a spry fellow! How he ever snared Maggie was a big mystery. He had a few children by a first marriage, one of whom visited him from England for a holiday. She intrigued me as she always referred to a sunny day as 'the weather is fine today'. I didn't know what 'fine' meant. In later years Frank left Maggie and retired to the Seychelles with another woman.

There were others in my parents' group of friends; Dr and Mrs Ward who may still live in Que Que (if they are alive), and the now deceased Dr Hirsh and his wife, a woman whom I never met, who lived next to the Globe and Phoenix Club. There were the Vermeulens, a Canadian couple. He was the manager of the Roasting Plant. We used to visit them quite frequently. They had a large house on a hill with the ubiquitous mosquito netting all the way round their veranda. I recall the bougainvilleas, frangipani and the rock gardens, because the garden was steeply tiered, with a view looking north over the town. We liked swimming, in the pool at the plant (that is Redcliff Steel Works), which was a long way from their house, and where we would swim our little hearts out for hours on end, from morning until late afternoon, ducking and diving into the cool, green, chlorine depths. We would emerge red-eyed and start all over again. Later, when completely drained of energy we lay on the warm concrete surrounds until dry. Later when the Vermeulens moved away Mrs Vermeulen, (Peggy), said that leaving Que Que meant that, 'The world would be *ourroyster*'. I did not know what a 'royster' was and could not understand how anyone's world could be that thing with such a peculiar name. We never heard from them again.

Mum was also friendly with the Massons and the Elsworths who farmed out of town. (In the latter case Mrs Elsworth always addressed Mum as 'Mrs Hakkie'). She flattered her outrageously, comparing me to my mother. Every time she came to visit she would exclaim loudly,

'Why Mrs Hakkie you look as young as Borgie'.

I hated the comparison and glowered. Some Sundays we visited their farm, the house set way up on a rocky outcrop. I distinctly recall hearing 'The Desert Song' with Janette McDonald and Nelson Eddy, and falling in love with the music. Mrs Elsworth was putatively a cordon bleú cook, but Mum said her food was 'execrable and uneatable'.

Years later my mother told me that their son Henry[8], whom I regarded as utterly gorgeous, was in love with her. I was shocked. (I looked at Mum — who could be in love with her, she was so old!) Whether this was true or not is hard to know as was decidedly vain in her younger days. In due course Henry married and had a family. He came to a sticky end, poor man, being gunned down (see footnote). There were two other families who lived near the Massons, the Richardsons and the Van Rynevelds. These three families lived in a section of Que Que across the golf course. I walked along a path amongst tall trees to visit Claire van Ryneveld, whose name I thought was the most beautiful name I had ever heard. She was a blonde pretty open-faced little girl,

---

[8] Henry Elsworth was gunned down outside his farm during the so-called land reform takeovers in 2001, as perpetrated by the Mugabe Government.

but I do not remember her parents or her sister. In the case of the Richardsons – Mr Richardson was the manager of Barclays Bank, his wife Nora had false teeth with very orange-coloured gums which fascinated me. Sometimes we visited Nora and I would stand and stare at her clacking teeth with the crazy gums. Once I said: 'Why do you have orange in your mouth?' (referring to her gums).

I compounded the peccadillo by telling her that, 'One of our hens is named Nora, after you, because it is so fussy pecking about!'

Mum was furious and never forgave me. She was talking about what a terrible child I was saying that to Mrs Richardson even when we were living in Australia. I wonder why she was surprised! What did she think would be the outcome of discussing her friends in front of her children?

Apart from all the people she disliked in Que Que, Mum had other prejudices, she didn't like the Japanese, because she said she remembered what they did during the war, and besides which 'they treat animals very badly'. No doubt all of this was true but to us it meant nothing. Dad on the other hand, was decidedly anti-semetic. He spoke about 'Ikeys' and believed that every shop that caught fire was set alight by a Jew so that he could cash in the insurance! However, they were respectful of the Slomans, two local Jewish families, who had the town's General Store. Their intelligence was a given, they had money and a certain standing in the town. But, although I was friendly with Eileen, the Slomans were never invited to our home.

— 4 —

Life with our Servants and the Village School

Although our servants formed a most important background to our lives, had we been asked about them, or thought about their place in the scheme of things, we'd have said they were just there to do our bidding. But, the truth was, we could not do without them.

The most important person in the organisation of our home, (we hardly registered this at the time), was Esther, a bony, spare, coloured woman, my mother's maid and nanny to the children. Mum insisted she wore a white apron and bonnet, in the style of English servants. She lived somewhere other than on our premises, I have no idea where, and had a girl child of her own. I saw her daughter a couple of times, thin like her mother, with her crinkly plaits; she was several years older than I.

Esther's life must have been hell, I know I gave her a difficult time. She worked long hours, as did most servants in Southern Rhodesia. She bathed, fed and looked after us, babysitting when our parents went out at night. I think she made the beds, did the washing and ironing, but really I was so unaware of what went on domestically, maybe one of the other servants did these chores. I used to kick up a hell of a stink if Esther wanted me to come home at 5pm, our deadline, (especially if I was playing with junior school boarders), when bathing and dinner was the order of each day. I bit and scratched her on occasions. Sighing a lot, and sometimes looking bored, she took it all mostly with equanimity, or at least never showed her feelings of humiliation. She was with us for many years.

Then there was Campbell, who seemed always to be smoking. We used to call him 'scrambled eggs'. (His surname was Zuzu.) Campbell did not speak to us very often, probably given instructions not to. Middle-aged, with a balding head and a grizzled appearance, he wore khaki shorts with a red stripe down each side, and did the basic cooking like breakfast ('blekkfist is ready', he would say), a white apron tied round his stocky body, which emphasised his bow legs. His complexion was dark and he had a neat moustache.

He often cooked guavas for us on the little wooden stove outside the back door. We'd relish the burnt skin which seemed to make the fruit sweeter.

Special meals were left to Mum. Her meat pies and lemon pudding were wonderful, pastry just perfect, the lemon pudding a lemony, sugary, cakey concoction. She was a 'pioneer' in Rhodesia because she made spaghetti bolognaise at a time long before the Italians built Kariba Dam and brought their cuisine to the philistines! As the years went by she taught Campbell a lot more about cooking, and he became adept at this skill. We were considered good eaters and consumed most of what we were given, but if not, 'Think of the starving children in the East'. We had not a clue, nor did we care about starving children in the East, or anywhere else for that matter.

Campbell was accommodated on our premises in the servants' quarters at the back fence, right next to the garage, and he stayed with us a long time too.

Richard was our houseboy, the memory of whom is vaguer. He had an upright figure and was quite pale-skinned. He was much younger than Campbell, a shadowy figure who cleaned, polished silver and shone the red granolithic veranda on his hands and knees. He would dab on the red, slippery polish from a wide-mouthed metallic tin and then rub for all he was worth, humming to himself in a particular rhythmic African way, I can still visualise the soles of his feet as he laboured on all fours. He shone our shoes every morning and maybe ironed, as most male domestics did. I cannot remember whether or not I ever exchanged a word with him. He stayed in our employ until Mum left us. I regret I have no photographs of these tireless workers in our home.

Mum's attitude to her servants was one of ambivalence. She did not trust them and locked all the provisions away in the pantry. She wandered around with a large bunch of keys attached to her belt, which jangled as she walked and which she invariably mislaid, 'Where are my keys?' this said plaintively, then more stridently, 'Who has my keys?' Esther invariably told Mum where her keys had been left. Then Mum would complain that the servants were stealing her sugar. 'They'd steal you blind, these people', she'd say. This was not unusual in colonial Africa; the topic of conversation at many a coffee morning was how to keep one's groceries intact. Housewives, including Mum, secreted their groceries from what they perceived as the light-fingered Africans, who were always offended by these remarks and grumbled in their own lingo among themselves. What did they say? Probably something to the effect that we whites had so much sugar why should we resent if they took a little extra? And who could blame them?

Over the road from us, on the northern side of our garden, was the junior boarding house which was built in close proximity to the public school. It had green down-pipes and guttering on the white brick building. To my eyes it was a huge place with a dusty, grassless large garden, as extensive as our own, which had a three-strand wire, paddock-like fence. We quite often trudged across the dusty space to play with the young children there in the afternoons. Once the Brownies, to which I belonged, had a campfire in their grounds. We sat by the fire singing songs. One was 'Who Killed Cock Robin?' – my brother can still sing this in Zulu – and we learnt 'Kookaburra Sits in the Old Gum Tree'. Little did we know all those years ago that both Mum, John and I would land up in the country of kookaburra and kangaroo!

Village School

On weekdays Esther packed us something for tea break, placing these comestibles in our little school bags and sending us on our way. We crossed a dirt road to get there. Our school was a white painted building with black lettering 'Que Que Public School'. It seemed very large, with lots of trees and extensive gardens. It took pupils from age 6 years to 18 years of age, hence the need for the junior boarding school mentioned earlier.

Que Que school was built in a long ranch style which, at its northern end, suddenly went off at right angles, before creeping forwards again. The junior school rooms ran off an open veranda on the left as you faced the building. Opposite the entrance was a locker room with pegs to hang blazers, and then on the right, the assembly room. This room had shields of a lovely nut brown wood upon which all the names of the various teachers at the school throughout the years and those who had achieved sporting and academic fame were engraved. The middle classes and seniors' rooms proceeded along the open veranda up to a right-angle bend, at which point there was a bank of stairs going up to the right to a second floor with classrooms at the top. In front of the stairs was concrete for sports and a wall. An opening in the wall led to an attractive garden full of flowers.

The headmaster's and teachers' offices were set around this flower garden and then, more classrooms. It was nothing special as public schools go.

The only teacher I remember, apart from the headmaster (Mr Davidson?), a Mr Evans and Dr Fitch, was a Mrs Hodge, our class teacher. She was fierce with her wiry, crimped hair done up in a roll. Dumpy, she had a creased powdery face. She seemed to dislike the students.

'Borgie Hawkey, stop chattering away with Eileen, if you don't mind'.

She would bang the desk. 'Aaron Aronowitz, have I to tell you again to stop making paper darts'. (I visualise her thinking *'little brutes'*)

If she disliked us, the locally born children, we were all influenced by the suspicion and reticence which spread throughout that school towards the influx of British migrants and their children during the early 1950s. Many of these immigrants went to Salisbury and Bulawayo but some came to live in our backwater. They were regarded with contempt because they were 'Not like us'. 'Low class', Mum said, and as for their accents, they were beyond redemption. They talked funny! One little English migrant boy whose name I forget was in my class at school. I remember his socks were always rolled over his shoes, which were scuffed. He was fascinating, just like Richmal Compton's *Just William*. According to our teacher, he 'came to school, is unwashed and has a dirty neck and elbows. So, off you go and tell your mother not to send you to school in that *state*'.

He would regularly be sent home with a letter instructing his mother to get him cleaned up. I can see his shaven head hanging, conveying his despondency and rejection, as he slowly walked home kicking stones, stirring up eddies of dust. We had not, at that time, been exposed to different kinds of people. Then, horror-of-horrors, there was an outbreak of head-lice. Mum bought a comb with very fine teeth and religiously went through our hair looking for nits. We were clean she announced with satisfaction. Head-lice is not the scourge today that it was then. If you had lice you were regarded as something brutish. Implicitly we believed the lice crept on to the heads of those in our pristine society directly from those migrants! You could describe us as xenophobic; we rigidly followed the British class system, though, I am sure we were not consciously aware of why we behaved so badly.

But, when the bell rang at play-time all thoughts of being better than the new Rhodesians disappeared. We'd rush outside. Different girls got together playing Sevens, which was the craze. This was a curious game using a tennis ball. You used the ball in a sequence of seven movements: for example the first seven times the ball was bounced on the ground at an angle so that it flew against the wall. On its downward flight you were supposed to catch it. If you did that properly the second sequence might be throwing the ball against the wall and letting it bounce twice on the ground and then you caught it in a particular sequence. If you varied the order, say, the ball bounced once instead of twice, or you dropped the ball, or forget the correct sequence of events etc, you were *out* and the next girl would take your place. There were about five sequences of Sevens. For nimble and supple bodied children Sevens was no challenge at all. Along the part of the school buildings where there were no windows, was the *thump thump* of ball on wall or ground, accompanied by 'one, two, three, four, five, six, seven', intoned slowly. When the Sevens phase passed it was skipping. Here again there were different types of skipping; the rope held at both ends by two girls swinging it in a circular fashion over the participant's head, who tried to skip without entangling her legs. Sometimes another person would enter the skipping area, skirt flying, black shoes landing flat on the ground, she would skip a couple of times, and then leave and a third person would join in and so on. The boys meanwhile played marbles; their interest remained constant. They spent all their play-time trying to get bigger and better marbles from each other. If you got the lead 'goon' you were a champion beyond champs. They squatted in the dust, their khaki shorts and shirts and their black shoes slowly turning a dusty brown colour. They looked well-suited to the environment. Some boys did so well at marbles they had cotton bags chock-a-block full of their winnings. (Do boys still play marbles I wonder? Probably not with the enthusiastic ferocity of those days.) All too soon the bell rang and it was back to reading, writing and arithmetic.

I did badly at anything mathematical, but could read and write well. Dad used to say of me, 'If you gave her pounds, shillings and pence to multiply she came up with pints and gallons!'

Mum went through phases of trying to help me with my arithmetic homework, but gave up in despair as I invariably burst into tears. My lack of numeracy was a big problem and I felt I would never overcome it. To this day I believe I am mathematically dyslexic.

The junior years were great fun as our class rooms overlooked the bush on one side and a veranda led to the grounds on the other. It was light, airy and safe.

We had small brown desks with ink wells and I remember lots of chalk, the white and coloured dust of which flew about when rubbed off the board with the special pad used for that purpose. Writing and tables were drilled into us. We had to write very precisely. We were taught to form the letter 'e' with its upward stroke and a good rounded loop at the top. The 'h' a long straight line with a skinny loop at the top. Our teachers insisted we left a good space between letters and words and we got bad marks if the writing was crowded.

'Don't use the first line of your jotter; make sure there is a good margin on the side and on the bottom'.

If you did not obey this simple command our teachers used to get cross, scribbling in our books in red, carping about 'cramping'. They were obsessed with having the first line empty of writing. I never understood why. Children who could not read were treated as complete dunces, they got a *thwack* on the back of their knees. Perhaps they had dyslexia – no-one knew about that condition then. Poor kids!

Tables we learnt by rote, a mantra: 'One times seven is seven, two sevens are fourteen, three sevens are twenty-one, four sevens are twenty-eight, five sevens are thirty-five, six sevens are forty-two' and so on. This was not an unpleasant way to learn tables for you never forgot them. Figures also, were to be written in a certain acceptable way. The teachers corrected our spelling and grammar and untidiness was truly a venal sin!

As for history, we learned all about our dear leader Cecil John Rhodes, the 'founder of our nation'. Leander Starr Jameson was another 'pioneer' from those days, and we were told all about the Jameson Raid into Matabeleland – all truth of course was bleached out of the telling of the story, he being depicted a hero when he was not. Nothing was ever related about the true story of how the British under Rhodes snatched Matabeleland, as it was known then, and made it a British colony.[9] 'Perfidious Albion' (as Shakespeare puts it) operating at her greediest and most duplicitous. In fact we learnt nothing about our own history except that Lobengula was King of the Matabele and something about Mzilikazi. I didn't even know whether the latter was from Rhodesia or South Africa.

Dr Fitch tutored us in religious matters, where we learnt about the burning bush, Lazarus arising from his bed, the Crucifixion and Jesus ascending into Heaven. None of it meant a thing to me, for I did not possess the religious 'gene'.

Every morning we had mandatory PT[10] under a large tree in the school grounds and did a lot of running about. There were few fat children at our

---

[9] For an excellent account see *Rhodes* by Antony Thomas (1993)
[10] Physical training

school, and like schools all over the world we played sport, and had cricket fields and tennis courts. These courts backed onto the headmaster's home, and there were fields between it and our house. On my return to Zimbabwe in 1999, that same large grassy area with its huge tree was now filled in with government buildings and I found it difficult to map out exactly where everything had once been.

Although I had friends at school when I was young, some children did not like me, 'You are a show-off because your Dad is a magistrate'. They teased me jealously because he drove a brand new American Mercury. If I sat in the back of the Merk they jeered at school, 'Saw you yesterday. Is your father your chauffeur? Snob, snob, show-off'. I was a snob as far as they were concerned if I sat in the front too. There was no way out in Que Que in those days. I cringed from their prejudices.

I also wrote plays, illustrating all the characters. But I was not a happy child and this interfered with school work; my creativity never truly bloomed. I was probably a brat who reacted badly to my peers' criticism, although it felt to me as if I was misunderstood both at school and at home.

As I grew older things changed and I became friendly with Eileen Sloman, whose father and uncle owned Sloman's, an emporium selling everything one can imagine. It was a huge barn of a place opposite the Que Que Park. The interior was rather dark. Down one side you could buy bicycles, pumps, agricultural equipment and seeds of every description. There was a large haberdashery section with rolls and bolts of cloth of different widths and colours, buttons, thread, tailor's chalk, scissors. Everyone sewed in those days. The counters were wooden and left in their natural colour, as were the cupboards and other fittings. It was a prosperous place. Eileen's family lived in one of a few double-storey houses in the town; perhaps it was the only one. When I was older I visited Eileen quite a lot. Her elder brother Aaron was very keen on classical music and was intellectual and interested in philosophy. Once, when I was quite a lot older, Aaron asked what was to me an astonishing question: 'How do you know other people exist?' I chewed over that one for years. Eileen also had a fat sister called Rochelle but I had little to do with her.

When I was about 11 years-old, while on a family drive, it started to rain on the way home. I saw a black man standing under a tree in the bush sheltering himself from the downpour in his raggedy brown jacket, threadbare trousers and no shoes.

'Look Mum, that man is cold, see how awful his clothes are'.

Mum and Dad concurred this was an abomination.

This incident really bothered me. I rang my friend Eileen and told her all about this sodden African. We both agreed that this was terrible, and talked about it at school. In no time at all news got around the town that we favoured the blacks and we were called 'Kaffir lovers', which said it all. 'Kaffir lovers, Kaffir lovers', the kids jeered at us and we were shunned. Children can be very cruel.

I spent a deal of time on my own, reading at home. (I was a great reader, but was an isolated child). The incident about the African in the rain isolated me more than ever. I never confided in my parents about feeling left out at school. However, when I consider how I loathed the Catholic boarding school I was sent to later, Que Que Public School was a paradise, and after my abortive stint at the Bulawayo Convent at age 12, I was happy to return there.

I studied acrobatics and ballet, both of which I loved. In fact I was obsessed by the ballet and struck attitudes around the house, posing my feet in different ballet positions. Mum and Dad got fed up with my 'attitudes', *pliëas* and arabesques. At that stage in my life I believed I wanted to be a ballerina. I lapped up all the films on ballet and read glossy books from the library about dancing. As for the piano, I also attempted to play the instrument, but did not practice enough and at that stage was bored by it all. I hear the tick-tick-tick of the metronome, the irritation in the voices of the teachers I had, and despite their disapproval, today I regret I never pursued the mysteries of the piano. Mum convinced me that I never stuck to anything! That was a prescription to fail if ever there was.

– 5 –

How Did We Amuse Ourselves?

We enjoyed utmost freedom when we lived in Rhodesia in the forties and fifties. I can remember when I was about 10 years-old and John seven years that one of our favourite activities was playing tracking with the *piccanins*[11] from the local golf course. They lived with their parents in African huts with thatched roofs, or in some sort of tin-shed arrangement, and their fathers tended the 'greens'. I use the word lightly because this was a golf course whose 'greens' were made of sand! We got on very well with the African children, with their loud exuberant voices, their sun-shiny smiles splitting their black faces, and tattered clothes and holes in their *takkies*, if they had such things. Tracking was an exciting activity after summer rainfall. The piccanins were enthusiastic – tracking was something they excelled at. There were many muddy puddles and the bush seemed to hum and sing with all sorts of insects. The grass grew waist-high and the vegetation took on an intense green mantle. It was so very African, and, despite the bright sunlight, had a brooding atmosphere, a stillness punctuated by frogs and cricket noises. We, accompanied by Timmy, would draw chalk arrows on the tree trunks and leave parcels in odd places for trackers to find. We spent hours and hours tracking, an innocent way of amusing ourselves. We spent hours playing with *chongololos*, those black serrated wormy things. One touch and they dance about and then curl up tight. We waited until they uncurled and started all over again. They had many legs and were so unusual that we never tired of the game. Dung beetles, peculiar to Africa, were engaging, for they busily collected mounds of dung from the droppings of cattle and are not to be mistaken for the stink beetle which had a lingering sour, citrus smell if crushed underfoot. We certainly did not like them!

---

[11] Name given to African children

I was so unaware of our unbelievable safety, so much so that, after Mum and Dad separated and I was still living in the family home, I took to walking the streets late at night. I do not know why, maybe I felt resistant to danger; an unrealistic sense of freedom gripped my imagination. I'd arise from my bed, dress quickly and set out through the dark garden, out the front gate, past the pale street light on the corner, down the dusty road, through the traffic-circle, across the depression in the road over the small tributary where a single jacaranda tree dipped its droopy leaves, along the back streets, for I avoided the brightly lit main streets, and into town. No-one saw me, or if they did they never mentioned the fact. I was nigh on 12 years-old. Then I'd go home, by which time it was probably midnight. I gained something from these nocturnal activities – perhaps just because I could do this.

Despite the fact we literally lived in the heart of the Rhodesian bush, activities for the local kids were arranged by our teachers and parents. We did not attend as many parties as today's children, and in any event they were much simpler affairs. I can remember the piano teacher's party where I won a prize for the best drawing of an elephant. That was a thrill. I think she gave me a small ornament. But it was the Soap-Box Derby and Decorated Bicycle competitions that made the deepest impression.

Soap-Box Derby

Up the hill at the broadest point where three roads met, and next to the Anglican Church, was the place where the annual soap-box derby began. For weeks beforehand the local boys (girls were never involved) built their soap-boxes. There was great anticipation. Billy Van der Westhuizen's Dad, who was known as Van, or Mr Van, made the best soap-boxes, but Billy never won a race.[12] In fact he never even finished and was always crying, his hands rubbing his eyes, his head with the bristle-cut dun coloured hair, hanging low. On the other hand, another lad had won a couple of times by the time he was 9 years-old. He made his own soap-boxes, not very well. His father had died while out shooting game. Mostly the local fathers helped their 'all thumbs' sons. No-one would dream of buying a ready built soap-box.

---

[12] These names have been changed.

The soap-boxes were mostly of wood with small rubber-tyred wheels. A rope was attached to the steering contraption with some sort of braking mechanism. This hopefully meant the impact of tumbles would be minimised, for the declivity of the road meant the soap-boxes got up to quite a speed.

Every parent in Que Que, plus siblings, lined the street to watch this exciting (to us) event. There were coloured pennants, flags, balloons, piped music, all the paraphernalia of childhood events were specially created for the day. The sun shone, the skies cerulean blue. I never remember it raining on soap-box Derby Day. People perspired under the blue sky. The ice-cream boy in his white shorts and shirt, his black face dripping with sweat, with his cart-on-a-bicycle, sold out his ice-cream wedges within an hour or so.

'Ladies and gentlemen', a disembodied voice boomed from the tannoy, 'Welcome to the annual soap-box derby for 1949 (50, 51 and so on). Please remember to keep to the footpath so as not to impede the competitors'. More music, hits of the day: 'A-Tisket, a-Tasket'; the Andrews Sisters singing 'Drinking Rum and Coca-Cola'; American Civil War songs; 'The British Grenadiers'; an endless supply of toe-tappers.

'The first event will be the race for under-eights, so line yourselves up'.

We did not know or care who won the under-eights, we were interested in the under-tens, because those boys were in our class at school. And shortly the starter announced the race for the under-tens.

The boys lined up, the metal part of the wheels scraping the bitumen, then 'bang' from the starter's gun and they were off. No-one wore crash hats then. With a trundling, rattling and spinning a dozen or so soap-boxes got under way. A huge shout emanated from the crowd. 'Bet that Billy van der Westhuizen crashes his cart again', said Ricky Aronowitz. We all expected that would happen, so no-one disagreed.

'Go Mark!' 'Giffy!' 'That's my boy Anthony!' Screams from parents and the children amid much clapping.

'Billy, Billy, hold the ropes straight!' yelled a frustrated Mr Van. 'Oh! No!' His arms in the air, as predictably Billy's race ended in tears and a scraped and bloodied knee, as he fell into the gutter and his vehicle splintered against the kerb. Giffy Evans[13] won the race in his soap-box which looked as if it were stuck together with tape and string.

---

[13] Name changed.

At the end of the race others took their place, the under 12s, 14s, 16s and so on. Throughout the morning wheels fell off, brakes failed, boys crashed into the paving, cried, fell out of their contraptions, blubbed – a gorgeous chaotic scene. From out of the mêlée emerged the inevitable winners, the first to cross the STOP line on the flat. What then did a few broken teeth, grazed knees, blood noses, shattered boxes matter when you could win chocolates, packets of biscuits, a book token, toffees – bliss!

After all the excitement, at about 12 o'clock the fathers, their shirts stained under their armpits, repaired to the Que Que Hotel. Mums, dusty and anxious – and who wouldn't be – took their bruised and bloodied children home to tend to their wounds, with their carts, if salvageable, in tow. Mr Van was seen in his red lorry, the broken soap-box in the back and a dejected Billy, blanched, sitting at his side. Maybe next year they'd do better.

A trail of ice-cream wrappers stirred in the indolent breeze and sticks, cold drink bottles, not to mention the broken wooden planks, wheels that had fallen from cross bars and other bits and pieces were left to be cleaned up by the Africans employed so to do. Soap-Box Derby Day was over for another year!

Decorated Bicycles

In direct contrast to the soap-box derby was the decorated bicycles competition. This was a demure affair where the only thing that got broken, temporarily, were children's hearts. All of us with bikes were encouraged to beautify them. Either that, or to think up something novel and interesting in the decoration of their bicycles. Bikes were black in those days with gold lettering (they may have been a Phillips brand), not enameled in the bright colours of today. Black was a good contrast for decorations.

We assembled in the vacant lot behind the large advertising hoarding next to the Town Clerk's office. A few doughty souls rode to the venue through town. Some came in cars, their bicycles strapped to the back, or else they were in trucks and lorries in which case the bikes were piled into the tray. Just about every kid in Que Que made their way there.

'My Mum is decorating my bike with crêpe paper flowers and bows', said Eileen. Little did she know most of the bikes were like that, for Priscilla Tarr and Jean Bradley, who decorated their own bikes, favoured this style. Maybe it was just that this was the easiest for them or their mothers to make. However, there was a variation to the theme, for many had coloured crépe strips wound around the handlebars and cross bars. And those who really wanted to impress had spokes dressed up, or wheels covered over. It was a plethora of pink, yellow, green, red, blue crépe paper.

One year I entered my own bicycle into the competition. Within five minutes of arriving at the judging point the paper on my bike began to unravel and float slowly off into the breeze. Other hapless children impotently tried to fix their wrecked decorations as sticky tape or brown tape came away from the rough surface of the crépe. Then I noticed the bike slightly behind but next to mine. It was a gorgeous confection; the handle bars had yellow butterflies tied every two inches or so. The same butterflies were tied to the spokes, five to each. From the saddle was a piece that curved around the rider's back at an angle of about 60 degrees from the body. This was festooned with streamers, woven pieces filling in the space giving it a sort of basket-like texture and appearance. Each piece was woven with green, blue and yellow crépe paper. The cross bar had bands of matching colours. Oh! It was magnificent.

I did not know the child, had never seen her before. I stared at her and she, catching my eye, looked gravely back at me. Short brown fringe, a green and white dress in *broderie anglais*, with pale green pearl buttons, pale green socks and white shoes made up her ensemble. And in her hair, yellow butterflies. I was mute – that such a bike and such a child should live in our community! I looked at my pink bows on the handlebars of my bike, the limp, long lost streamers which were supposed to be around the cross bars, and my general untidiness. A feeling came over me rather like that which the author Milan Kundera describes as *litost,* a desire to spite the other because one feels so inadequate. I wanted to hit out, lie down on the hard stony ground, drum my heels, scream, scratch – for I was that sort of child. I did none of those things, at least not there, but I took out my frustrations later, when Esther wanted me to get into the bath.

We wheeled our bicycles past the judges. They smiled, looking intent and interested, inspecting every confection and then – of course: 'The winner today, by far the best decorated bike and best presented child... Miss Butterfly'.

I do not remember who got the prize for the most novel bike, it didn't matter, Miss Butterfly had surpassed us all.

•

When I was a teenager, about 15-years-old, I returned to live in Que Que with Mum and my new step-father Tony. Our pastimes then were similar to those of other teenagers. We swam a lot at the local pool, which by this time was newly built. We went on picnics to the Sebakwe dam.

In 1999 during our visit to Zimbabwe, my daughter, her partner and I wanted to visit the Sebakwe dam. A smartly dressed guard told us it would cost us $US25 for the privilege. We politely declined, deciding to eat our picnic lunch on the grass outside the entry booth. This caused consternation – several Africans came to investigate what we were doing and trying to fathom why. We had noticed that for local Zimbabweans the price of entry was quite reasonable and explained our dissatisfaction. They retreated grumbling among themselves, with many 'Ehs' and 'Hows!'

One of our friends was Hugh Nangle, whom we called 'Hewn Ankle'. Then there was Jean Bradley and her gangly brother Ross, Lindy Jones, a great friend of mine, Eileen and assorted young men with whom we 'hung out'. Our favourite spot was The Chanticleer, a café with the latest in outdoor umbrellas, red and white striped. It was situated on the edge of town on the Salisbury road close to the pink flowering oleanders on the grass verge. We'd meet each other and walk up to The Chanticleer. There we drank milkshakes, ate copious amounts of Knickerbocker Glories, a confection of ice-cream, sauces, fruit and nuts. Unlike today's teenagers we knew nothing about drugs. We knew vaguely that Africans smoked *dagga* (marijuana). We pitied them; we heard they sat around looking dopey after smoking, but this aspect never entered our lives. My children find this incredible. 'What ma, you've never even had a drag? How very *Victorian*'. I remember reading about Sigmund Freud and opium and that certain aristocratic women in Europe took laudanum, but really had no idea what laudanum was, probably some sleeping draught. We were pretty innocent compared to young people today, but knew we were '*not to get pregnant!*' That was Mum's greatest fear.

Mum's favourite saying was that 'There is nothing in the world worse than an ungrateful child'. She had a Victorian sentimentality about love and devotion, and how one's children should revere their parents. She was never a feminist. Mum expected that if she entered a room and there was a man there, he should rise to his feet. If not, she gave the guilty one her 'evil eye'. Her belief in how children should behave, even when adults, did not modify with time. Deep down my mother believed men were superior. She once explained to me that her mother had said to her, in relation to her brother Gordon, 'Do it (ironing or whatever) for Gordon, he's a man you know'. Her generation (she was born in the early nineteen-hundreds) relied so much on men and their good opinion. I don't think she liked women; perhaps we would have had a better relationship if I had been born a boy. I might have received a kiss or two, as Mum only kissed those of the male gender! She never let on that her life was less than perfect with Dad. I realise now that she was putting on a good face about her crumbling marriage, but she hid the truth well. Even in her 90s she was as indomitable as she had always been, with a fine intellect. She discussed politics, history, societal ideas and knew a lot about many things, especially history: things like the English Monarchy, the French Revolution, the Napoleonic wars and British history down the ages. She made all the curtains in our Rhodesian homes, painted, was a good cook, and decorated everything marvelously. Get her on a good day she was witty, with an attractive sense of humour. She had the knack of finding apt names for people which was both devastating and hilarious. For example, when I lived in Sydney, a very fat lady of our acquaintance visited wearing a shiny pink outfit. Mum immediately dubbed her 'the pink blancmange', as she was, 'Wobbling along, looking for all the world like a pink blancmange on the move'.

A friend said, 'Your mother is funny in an unexpected way, as long as one is not the butt of her acerbic wit'.

My own children loved it when the family got together. After Gran had two glasses of wine (which was a lot for her), she'd giggle spontaneously, her irrepressible child emerging for a few minutes, only to be tucked away again.

– 6 –

The Royals come to Town, 1947, and Holiday in Fish Hoek, 1948

One day when Dad came home from work, I could tell because of his purposeful walk that he was excited. He hugged Mum and gave her a big smacking kiss on her cheek.

'Pat, we're getting a royal visit. The King, Queen and Princesses are coming here. Can you believe it?' Mum was suitably impressed.

'Well', she said, 'I'll have to make a new outfit – when are they coming?'

Dad mentioned the date. It was in 1947. We were on the route of the Royal Tour of the colonies. John was too young to realise the import of this bit of news; nevertheless he wandered around clapping his chubby hands saying, 'King's coming, King's coming'. For we colonials this was a momentous occasion, particularly as we lived in a backwater and anything different was of great excitement.

At school the next day we were told the good news at assembly.

'All the Scouts, Guides, Brownies and Cubs are to wear their own uniforms on the great day', said the Headmaster. As can be expected there was an outbreak of chattering.

'Quiet!' He had to raise his voice. 'No talking until assembly's over – now let us say our daily prayers'. (That's what they did in those days).

After assembly we broke rank and continued the chattering. All that morning and the following weeks we were apprised of our particular roles. The King, Queen and Princesses were arriving in the royal train. They would meet local dignitaries (we had a few) and drive past the townsfolk who were to meet in the park close to the railway station. The Brownies, of whom like all the other little girls in the village, I was one, were to assemble in our packs, and Brown Owl would line us up to wave at the Royal family. Meanwhile Mum was frantically making herself a wine red outfit.

Esther too was excited. 'Heh!' she said, 'The King is coming to see us', with great emphasis on the 'us'. 'What an honour'. She had an enthusiastic look in her black eyes. Our cook, Campbell, had little to say. He sat outside the kitchen door on the gravel smoking.

'Do you think it's exciting?' I asked him.

He grunted, 'What name Princesses, where from?'

I told him, 'Elizabeth and Margaret' and that they came from overseas 'England', I said.

'Ah Ingrind'. He looked thoughtful, 'Where Ingrind?' I was stumped and kicked the gravel, 'Overseas', He stared at me and continued smoking, his grizzled countenance more puzzled than usual.

Meanwhile the Town Clerk and other dignitaries had arranged for extra street sweeping and cleaning at that time, even painting was undertaken where necessary.

The station gleamed pristine, white, sterile, but nothing could be done about dust. It was late autumn and there had been no rain for months. That was what the Midlands weather was like. Therefore, dust eddies swirled in the slightest breeze, the sky, a baked enamel, crisp, cold enough for a fire at night, but a warm 20° by day.

'Why have they chosen this time of year?' the locals grumbled, 'It is so dry and dusty. What will they think?'

Eventually the great day was upon us. Everyone who was anyone in the town was lined up, all looking their best and full of anticipation for the occasion. The local Africans climbed trees for a view. I heard them scrambling and shouting to one another in their exuberant way. Some, in their excitement, fell from the branches. This accompanied by a yell and much laughter from their friends. 'Heh King' and then they would break into their own language, foreign to our ears. We never learnt Shona, Chikarunga, Zulu, Xhosa, Indabele – name it, most whites were impervious to them all.

We waited, the sun was hot, it was dry, the dust lay dormant on a windless day. The Scouts chatted idly amongst themselves. All around me children stood waiting patiently. A rumour ran through the crowd, 'They've changed their minds!'

'Rubbish', said Brown Owl, 'they'll be here pretty soon'. We weren't convinced and started murmuring.

'Do you know the train is gold plated?' said one of the Brownies.

'Really?' This was electrifying news to us. We stared bug-eyed.

'Yes', she said, pleased with all the attention, 'And they have lots of people doing things for them'.

'What sort of things?' Ricky Aronowitz wanted to know.

'Oh, you know', she said, caught on the hop, 'Ironing, cooking...' Her voice trailed off. We, who never ironed an item in our lives and certainly never cooked, lost interest. Ricky started punching his friend; boredom crept insidiously through the ranks.

Then suddenly, there they were — the entourage, men in helmet-style headgear with flowing feathers, a possé of cars and then George, Elizabeth and the two Princesses passed. They looked cross but waved nevertheless. Poor Royals, they must have loathed it, constantly bathed in a fine dusty patina. I can imagine George and Elizabeth thinking that 'Que Que was a god-forsaken place'.

We screamed, up came the flags - red white and blue, we waved our Union Jacks. It all happened so quickly and before long, they were gone. All we had as a reminder was a commemorative stamp of the great occasion.

Years later I saw a black and white film of the Royal Visit to Rhodesia and there I was, brown socks, Brownie uniform, hair straight in those days, cut in a fringe, yelling my head off. A curious nostalgia gripped me. I remember the helmets, the cars and two young girls - our Royal family; but was it worth all that preparation for a minute or two of a Royal visit?

When King George VI died on 6 February 1952, Dad was the first person in Que Que to know of the event. Naturally he told us too. I ran from one child to the other. 'The King's dead, The King's dead'. I felt very important because I was able to tell all and sundry, teachers included, that our King had died and that Princess Elizabeth would now be our new Queen.

The whole town mourned the passing of a well-loved Monarch and hoped the new Queen would cope with her new role, particularly as she was so young.

Dad's Parents, Fish Hoek Holiday, 1948

My father's parents were temperance people. Gran Hawkey, who was a cheerful soul, used to sing, 'My drink is water bright, water bright, water bright. My drink is water bright from the crystal stream'.

They were Cornish born, from Newquay, and I never tired of hearing how two brothers, Edward and Frank Hawkey married two sisters, Ellen and Ann

Goldsworthy. The men were tall and sinewy and the women cuddly, though Gran was fatter, and both of them wore glasses. They all had an attractive 'brrr' in their speech. My father was an only child with only one male cousin whom I met once. In the Cape my grandparents owned and ran a boarding house at the sea in Fish Hoek, Cape Province, called Hotel Lanark. Ann and Frank worked with my grandparents at the Lanark. Why this was so I do not know, it was just an accepted fact[14]. When I was about 9 ½ years-old, John and I once spent a three-month holiday at the Hotel Lanark, and it is one of two holidays I recall from my childhood. It was 1948, and our mother was going on a trip to the United Kingdom (another mystery we never asked about). As Rhodesia is a land-locked country Mum's ship sailed from Cape Town which meant a train trip from Que Que to the Cape.

•

What an exciting adventure for two country children. As the train is departing at night, we arrive dressed in our pyjamas with Mum. At Que Que station, a white board informs us in black stencilling that Que Que is '6,000 ft above sea level', which everyone says is a great elevation! I am almost sick with anxiety at the delicious thought of the three night and four day trip ahead of us.

Here's the train with its Rhodesia Railways RR logo etched into every window and painted on the side of every carriage, stationary at the platform. I do not know where our father is. (In fact he arrived in Fish Hoek about two months or so after we got there). I am not concerned with the details because once aboard, I am utterly fascinated by the little hand basin with a tap you press down hard. True it was a little difficult to depress, but when achieved, the water is ejected and exits the basin with a most satisfying *whoosh* - literally down the gurgler. I spend a deal of time pushing the tap up and down, until Mum in irritation tells me to 'stop it or I'll slap you'. We have a first class carriage with green leather upholstery and brown polished wooden fittings with four bunks, which differentiates the first class from the second class which has six. The two top bunks intrigue us. There is a strap to hold if the train's motion is too violent, and above each are the racks for luggage. The upholstery has embedded covered buttons, which causes a slight puckering at the point of entry into the leather. Around the walls of the carriage are photos

---

[14] Later Grand and Grandad moved from the Cape to Southern Rhodesia where they had a boarding house called Baines Hall in Salisbury.

of beautiful parts of Rhodesia, scenes that appeal to tourists; the Victoria Falls, Inyanga, Sebakwe River, the Matopos. These are set behind glass, and each carriage I discover has a different set of pictures.

Soon after the train leaves Que Que, a coloured 'bedding' man (I have never seen a coloured man), knocks on the compartment door. I ask him how he does this, and he shows me a small tubular section of metal about 8cms in length and 1 cm in diameter which fits into a depression in the door handle. This metal tube is jiggled back and forth using small movements of the hand and wrist which results in a sharp tat-a-tat rapping sound. To me he is a curious-looking person, beige complexion, skinny with black curly hair and dark hooded eyes which catch the light and seem to sparkle. He turns his penetrating gaze upon each of us in turn as though wishing to remember us for the future. He speaks, rolling his 'rrrrs' in a strange heavily accented fashion which today I know to be peculiar to the people from the Western Cape. 'Bedding mussus?' He addresses my mother. She nods. In no time at all he's made up three beds, two on the bottom bunks and one on the top. With a wide, rather ingratiating smile he leaves shouting a breezy 'Good night'. We brush our teeth, remove our dressing gowns and slip into our bunks. I have the top bunk, which causes an argument because my brother wants to sleep on the other top bunk.

'I want to sleep up there', says John. 'Why can't I sleep on the other top bunk?'

'You're too young and might fall out, so sorry you can't'. He demurs as he is a biddable child.

Throughout that first night I sleep fitfully. The train's whistle wakes me, the chugging and unfamiliar motion, the clatter when passing over a bridge or culvert, the noise of complaining metal under stress, the general excitement, stopping at towns and sidings. Although we have pull-down blinds, at large towns or cities, the lights on the station wake me. I hear people talking Afrikaans on the platforms at these unknown destinations. At other places I hear the clanking of rolling stock, shunting back and forth. But by early the first morning I have fallen asleep only to wake to the sound of 'Reveille' which we recognise as 'Come to the Cookhouse Door Boys' being played on a small xylophone by one of the waiters. It is time for breakfast! We are up and off to the dining saloon. Negotiating the narrow passages along the carriages is difficult as we are thrown from side-to-side by the movement of the train. Other passengers appear and it is fun to peer into the compartments when you espy an open door to see what other families are doing and what they look like. A man we would today call a *maitre d'hotel*, or *mein host*, meets us at the dining saloon door. Dressed all in black, at 7am, with a white shirt and bow tie, his side-parted Brylcreemed hair is as shiny as patent leather. He shows us to our places: both the table and benches are bolted to the side of the carriage, and you have to slide along the benches to get in. A crisp white cloth, a cruet set of glass with silver tops all rather battered, (certainly not shiny); of stainless steel, make up the placement. There are rather large fashioned cutlery and side plates all bearing the RR emblem which completes the setting. Mother gets hold of the menu and orders our breakfasts. When the meals arrive they are concealed in domed oval silver covers which the waiter removes with a flourish showing us the steaming food underneath – very impressive to a child. The stainless steel tea and coffee pots are so hot you can hardly touch them; and they drip all over the starched napery. The kitchen and waiting staff are mostly these 'coloured' people.

The toilets smell of urine and disinfectant. Passengers are admonished by a notice on the toilet wall not to use or flush the toilet while the train is stationary. Mother sings a little ditty, 'Passengers should please refrain from passing water on the train, when the train is standing on the station'.

She does not finish the couplet, it's as though she is embarrassed that she knows what she would describe as a 'vulgar song'.

The journey itself is one of hours of boredom, chugging along, very slowly. A joke – because a very Scottish gentleman on board says: 'Och! a passenger could nip off the train and pick the daisies [daisies in the Rhodesian bush?] and not get left behind'. We all laugh; how true it is. However, boredom is punctuated by exciting moments. We enter tunnels, everything turns black then with a flicker the lights come on. There are hills and ravines and when the track curves you get a view of the engine up front and can look back to see the guard's van, and sometimes the guard himself. What a great thrill! Only trouble is, we try in vain to avoid the gritty soot that streams from the gleaming black engine from getting into our eyes, without luck.

The brightness of the sun, the endless dust motes swirling, especially when the light catches them at a certain angle, plus the thin patina of soot that lies on everything, was synonymous with train travel then.

We cross the Rhodesian border at Plumtree and shortly the excitement of Francistown in Bechuanaland, a British protectorate in the 1940s. Today it is called Botswana and is home to the Tswana people. We enter the station which has a large green creeper over a grubby whitewashed building at which point the train finally comes to a stop with a sigh, almost as though it has a life of its own. Many of the locals gather to watch the train pull in. Dozens of African children and the odd old crone come running along the track, then up and down the train with carvings of animals for sale. Some have already been set down in anticipation of our arrival. Elephant, antelope, buck, hippos and giraffe carved out of pale wood with eyes and markings burnt into the flesh, or in the case of the elephants, in hardwood with mostly the thorns from the thorn trees which dominate the landscape, for tusks.

'Madam, Madam', a poor old crone, a tatty blue-and-white scarf wound around her head, beseeches my mother. 'Look Madam', she points to a beautifully carved wooden elephant. 'Only five shillings'. All along the track black children, most of them boys, stretch out their grimy hands, flies cluster in the corners of their eyes, snotty noses, torn khaki shorts, mostly they are barefooted, sell their wares. We bargain for these curios. Mum buys the elephant and another intricately carved piece. Today I cringe at how cheaply we got their artefacts.

People use the cliché – 'a colourful sight' – it is not that: energetic, dynamic yes, but mostly dusty and brown-hued. The sandy soil, heat, enamel blue sky, the steam from the engine, the shouts, the children and their animals, are imprinted in my imagination as being so African. This is an Africa we colonials were insulated from. We had a rigid fear of letting go and absorbing the life of the indigenes that pressed upon us so insistently.

Soon we say goodbye to lively Francistown and after an interminable time (where spacial reality and time has blurred) places like Gaberone and Kimberley, the names a roll-call from historical episodes. They are shown on the map as part of that railway, but are not remembered from that journey. Did we go through Mafeking, the relief of which is at the core of every South African schoolchild's history lessons? When did we cross the Orange River? Maybe we passed through these places at night, or I have forgotten, but we find ourselves in the Karroo, that endless flat desert country. The little towns have names like Laingsberg and Beaufort West. And then, the final part of our journey through the Hex River Mountains to Cape Town. Just to get through the mountains and descend to the Hex River Valley requires a special diesel engine which we picked up in De Aar (meaning the vein), and as suggested, is a rail junction of some importance. Gradually the topography changes. Gone is the dusty Karroo, the thorn trees, the endless blue skies. Here now are the renowned mountains of the Cape Province and clouds, some wispy, others piling cotton wool balls upon one another. Vistas open up. On one side runs the mountain wall and on the other a view across the valley. Endless vineyards, farms and market gardens, trees and orchards mark this fertile and well-cultivated area. When the train lurches into Worcester I am impressed at how different it looks from any town I have ever seen, with its Cape-Dutch houses and civic buildings. After a short stop it's on again to Paarl and the mountains which soar into the horizon. Everything about the Cape run is fascinating; the suburban trains we pass, the manner in which they whistle, the way the train rushes through the stations of the endless suburbs, the click-clack as we cross bridges and viaducts, and finally with a metaphoric aspiration, the arrival at Cape Town station where Gran, with her hat pulled over her brow, and Grandad in his tweed sports jacket – pale brown and cream – wait expectantly.

By now I am again in a state of anxiety, my life-time affliction, so much so the journey to Fish Hoek is like a dream. But on arriving at the Hotel Lanark, I am taken to a room. Cool it is, with a door with a rounded glass top surrounded by wood. I can hear the sea and smell the spray. And so I spend my first night of what turns out to be a magical holiday. John has his own room somewhere else in the hotel, but I am too engrossed in what is going on around me and I never know where it is. This may seem strange because we spend most of every day together!

The Lanark is open plan downstairs, with the dining room on the left as you enter and a large lounge leading off the foyer on the right. It has a central staircase to a landing from which you walk, either left or right, to the rooms at the top of the stairs. These rooms are sought after as they face the ocean and my grandparents have one of them; a double room with a small annex, with blinds, it is screened from the weather by wire netting. Simonstown, the naval base, is two stops on the train around the point from Fish Hoek. At night we hear the blast of the Simonstown fog-horn. I imagine Simonstown covered in fog, swirling, the mists hiding skulking reprobates, just like the atmosphere in Dickens' novels. Anyhow, this eerie sound epitomises Fish Hoek and the holiday for me.

Grandad and John, outside Lanark Hotel, c. 1948

Some of the rooms run at right angles around the sides of the Hotel Lanark building, and a granolithic open staircase takes one to the back concrete yard, which has a few pots and seaside plants dotted around its perimeter. Here the bedrooms are at ground level opening on to the yard at the back too.

The hotel is filled with elderly people, one in particular I remember, a Miss Chilcott, stern, white-haired and terribly old and thin who upbraids us because either my brother, father or I sat in 'her' chair in the lounge. She infuriates Dad who calls her an 'old harridan'. He deliberately tries to annoy her, with great success. She has been there for many years and feels that she is entitled to 'her spot 'and that we upstarts be put in our place! (no pun intended). The other elderly folk are tolerant enough. One night we put on a play for the guests, which as I recall, was all about sheets and much giggling; the landing on the top of the central stairwell being the stage. The oldies sit there bemused and clapping politely at the end. I was swollen headed with success and want to do other plays, but my grandmother diplomatically puts paid to that idea.

Fish Hoek station is almost right in front of the Lanark, and you need to cross the railway line without stepping on its central electrified cable to get to the beach. Fish Hoek is on the warm ocean side[15], and the land on which the town stands was donated by Lord Charles Somerset in 1818 (who was 'TT' according to Dad, which he told us means he did not drink alcohol), on the condition that there be 'no wine house on the property'[16]. The houses in Fish Hoek straggle up the hill in tiers so most people have ocean views. The town itself is unpretentious, filled with holiday makers, pedestrians of every hue, all wanting the warmth of the sun. The strange accent of the Capies[17] ring out on every corner. They laugh showing their toothless gums and chip each other in merriment.

This year the Cape has an Indian summer, an idyllic time for us. Every day the skies are cerulean, calm and the weather is hot. We spend three months, mostly on the beach, swimming and running. I have a new gold bubble costume – one of those elasticized cozzies stitched all over which takes on a bubbly appearance when unworn, a bit like crinkled bubble wrap. The mother of one of our holiday friends takes a movie of me frolicking in the sea wearing the gold bubble cozzie, which she promises to send to us, but she never does.

The beach at Fish Hoek is long and broad with white sand at the end of which are rocks reaching around to Sunny Corner. We play in the rock pools, trying to catch the slippery little silver fish that frequent the shallows. The water is the palest blue with foam left over from the waves rushing in and out. The rocks are a trifle slippery, so we step gingerly and poke twigs into anemones, orange and blue, their fronds close very quickly it seems; and we collect small shells. Being children we easily befriend and are befriended by other children on holiday who join us in our play. I am fascinated by the seaweed with its slimy brown branches and gold bobbles which are strewn across the beach after a high tide. We love picking up the branches and snapping the bobbles in our fingers.

Across the road from the beach and next to the Lanark is a tea room-cum-café, with windows almost to the ground, rather unusual in those days. We

---

[15] Indian Ocean
[16] This is still the case.
[17] Slang name for those of mixed race.

walk on the tiled, cool pavement and on entering the café we buy ice-creams – three scoops which sit side-by-side in the wide-mouthed cones; a triple decker of strawberry pink, white vanilla and chocolate. It's difficult to get them down without their melting, so we lick the sides in a frenzy to take up the oozing ice-cream, but mostly we fail in our endeavours. The owner gets to know us well and always welcomes us. Apart from ice-cream I am besotted with Peppermint Crisp, manufactured by Rowntree. My grandmother, from time to time (but not as often as I like) gives me a *tickey* (threepenny bit) to buy Peppermint Crisp. I run to the shop to buy my favourite chocolate, then to the back of the hotel where the cars are parked. I sit on the aluminium rail with anticipation, and slowly peel away the green silvery paper which sticks slightly to the chocolate. Sucking the chocolate deeply I stick my tongue into the jagged peppermint, full of holes, crunchy with pointed edges. I still like Peppermint Crisp but it is not the same as it was in 1948.

Sometimes, after Dad arrives from Rhodesia to join us, we move away from the beach café to the road behind the hotel, where reposes the Green Parrot Café. They have a genuine green parrot which fascinates us as we had never seen parrots before. This one cocks its head to one side, glares at us balefully out of its unblinking yellow-rimmed eye, ruffles its green feathers and squawks, 'Pretty Polly, Pretty Polly, Pretty Polly urk'. I think he is a stupid creature but he is quite an attraction, especially to all the local kids.

Grandad and Dad, outside Lanark Hotel, c. 1948

When grandmother or grandfather shop in the city, they never take their car but go by train. Once we are there, Gran buys what she needs and often buys John and me a little gift, and we generally finish up at Ansteys in Adderley Street, gravitating to the café/tearoom. There we have tea in a silver teapot with matching hot-water jug and are offered lots of small iced cakes yellow, pink, blue and white, of every shape from the display on a large trolley.

Naturally, we go with our grandparents on the train. We adore taking the brown-carriaged suburban train which runs from Simonstown through to Cape Town central. I know the name of every station along the route, and recite them in order which runs like a mantra through my head. I love the sound of 'Rondebosch', it rolls off the tongue and is my favourite name. Salt River intrigues me too, it being a place where a dreadful train crash occurred in the early 1940s. This story (which has gone into legend) is surrounded by rumours and tales of presentiments. Someone supposedly dreamt of a huge plane crashing into her home the night before. The dream being so vivid she did not take her usual train to work the next morning, or maybe she did not take her usual train home again. Others swore they had known people who had each seen the crash in a vision at the very hour it occurred. I can't get enough of the stories. But I digress: The commuters on the train are of enormous interest – all colours travelling together irrespective of their ethnicity, this is the Cape province's way in the late '40s! The carriages in trains and on suburban buses have signs reading Moenie Spoeg Nie or Do Not Spit, the letters set in a red ring. A round trip on the train from Fish Hoek to Cape Town takes about 50 minutes and when you reach smoky Woodstock, you know you're nearly at your destination. The view as the train comes down to the city is spectacular, whitewashed Dutch gabled buildings and a shimmering sea, and there on the left sometimes you see Table Mountain, if it's not covered by its tablecloth of cloud.

Going the other way from Fish Hoek to Simonstown is a short but lovely trip, the railway built so that the train is exposed on one side to the sea. You can see the ocean is deep and I feel frightened by its impenetrableness and its dark and mysterious colour. The first stop after Fish Hoek is Sunny Corner which is visible from our hotel, followed by Glen Cairn, mostly unspoiled with its open spaces, sandy outcrops and succulent seaside shrubs and finally the naval base Simonstown where the wind constantly blows a gale. Simonstown is an elegant place with well-maintained whitewashed buildings, manicured lawns, a better style than normal of shops, well-dressed people, plenty of naval uniforms, gold braid, buttons, white shorts and shirts. It is still like that.

Dad at Fish Hoek c. 1948

I returned to Fish Hoek in the early 1990s and was saddened to find the old train line decrepit, unmaintained, with inconvenient ticket purchasing facilities, unkempt stations and used mostly by poor Capetonians. In an effort to make something of the scenic beauty, at the time of writing the City Fathers have put to use some of the carriages as a breakfast trip for tourists which, by all accounts, works well. But money is needed to upgrade this most gracious of public transport, to attract commuters of every stripe.

In the evenings after dinner we listen to the wireless. A favourite programme is 'Snoek Town Calling', a comedy half-hour, very Capetonian, redolent of the people, sounds and smells of this most interesting part of South Africa. I suppose it is no longer aired after all this time. On Sunday nights Grandma and Grandad listen to a religious hymnal 'Golden Showers' which they talk about a lot. I badger them to let me listen to this and once, as a great favour, they do. I feel let down! I do not know what I expect but there were not many hymns that I could understand, besides which I find them terribly dreary. Then, off to bed with the sound, the wind, the smell of the ocean, and another day filled with who knows what to look forward to.

There was only one unpleasant occurrence which had to do with sex. Fish Hoek has an array of beach boxes painted in a variety of colours, which are still there. I assume they are used for changing before swimming, but never knew if they were hired or owned in perpetuity. One day a new friend and I while wandering across the beach find ourselves parallel to the beach boxes and there a naked man stands shaking his penis at us. He says nothing, and we, giggling with embarrassment, run away. I never told anyone about this episode, and in those days little was heard about this sort of thing.

•

'*Oklahoma*, have you seen the musical *Oklahoma*?' This word 'Oklahoma' was bandied about by the hotel residents. Several of the long-termers have been to what they describe as 'a wonderful musical'.

'Ellen, you must take the children to *Oklahoma*', Aunt Ann says to Gran, 'Or at least take Borgs'.

'What is it?' I ask one of the women.

'A musical dear, with a beautiful hero and heroine, and it is set in America. The music is so catchy. There're songs like "Surrey with the Fringe on Top" and, "Oh What a Beautiful Morning"'. This person began trilling in her strong vibrato: 'Oh what a beautiful morning. Oh what a beautiful day. I've got a wonderful feeling everything's going my way'.

'Oh Ellen do go, you'll love it'.

And so it comes to pass that Gran takes me to *Oklahoma*. I don't know if John accompanies us. It is performed in Cape Town, and on the way to the theatre a street photographer takes a photo of grandma and me. (We fetched the photo the next time we were in the city. Sadly, I have it no more).

We go to the matinee. There are masses of people, lots of little girls in a variety of coloured organdie dresses with satin sashes, ribbons in their hair and black shiny buckled shoes. The boys wear suits, their hair parted and slicked. Very smart, I think. Gran makes me wear my best dress as well.

'Want a programme?'

'Please Gran, buy a programme'. Which she does.

We file into the half-lit stalls, the usherette looks at our tickets, and shines her torch so we can find our seats. There is much chatter and laughter. After a short wait, the lights are extinguished, the audience quietens and the orchestra plays the overture; the velvet curtains are drawn back and the show begins. How I love it. I follow the story of cowhands and farmers who are exhorted to be friends with each other: there is a beautiful, proud girl who sings 'Many a New Day', and a handsome boy. There are lovely costumes. The story is of nature, love and loss, good versus evil. Oklahoma is, I decide, the place I'd like to be. I too adore Curly and hate Judd, and do not feel sorry that 'Poor Judd is Dead'. And the music...the music, it lives in your head for days. Everything about it is wonderful.

At half-time we shuffle out and join the throng. Pushing through the crowd, Gran buys me an ice-cream wafer. Some people spill out onto the pavements, whistling and humming the catchy tunes which are so instantly accessible. After what seems an interminable time, the bells ring and it's back again for the rest of the show, which ends far too soon for my liking.

There have been many remakes of *Oklahoma*, both on stage, and cinema, and I have seen a few, but for me that production outshines them all.

After the first month at the Hotel Lanark Dad turns up, I do not know where he stays, I never saw the inside of his room if he was at the hotel and I imagine he stays elsewhere. But I know Dad goes out a lot. One evening after dinner he suddenly appears wearing a midnight blue suit. It is quite stunning for a man to have a blue suit. He announces to all of us he is going dancing. I often wonder what my grandparents think, but I am sure they are not pleased, for they are religious and rather narrow in outlook.

Soon after his arrival he takes us out in his car to interesting places, he drives to Chapman's Peak and Hout Bay. Once we went to the Cape Town Gardens, an extensive park with lots of flowers, oak trees and full of squirrels, both red and brown – all the red squirrels are gone now. It is a cold day and I am in a coat with a velveteen collar. With peanuts I feed a twitchy-nosed red squirrel. A newspaper man - probably from the *Cape Argus* - takes a photo of me and my brother which appears in the paper the next day. How excited we are. Everyone at the hotel comments upon this. We receive a lot of attention, at least for a few days. I associate these trips with the Andrews Sisters and in particular 'A Little Bird Told Me That You Loved Me' and 'Powder Your Face with Sunshine' for these tunes were playing on Dad's car radio on our way to the Gardens.

Too soon my mother returns from her overseas trip. I do not remember whether we went to the docks to meet her or not, as I have overlapping memories from my first trip overseas to England when I was 18 years-old on the Union Castle line, but I do recall she is a vision in a green suit and hat. We leap upon her. She is happy to see us, giving us each a hug, but is concerned we might spoil her ensemble, because she says, 'Don't do that, you'll ruin my outfit'. Dad looks cross.

I assume we stay on at the Lanark for a while but do not remember our return to Que Que, whether or not Dad drives us that long distance home, probably he did. Only the holiday retains a glow of happy memories to this day, especially my grandparents' unconditional love, for we do not see much of them after that.

Later Mum tells me she'd been to Huddersfield in Yorkshire to go through Aunt Minnie's goods and chattels. This Aunt, Mum tells me, was a hoarder *extraordinaire,* as I explain in the next chapter. Mum also says it took her weeks to sort through the mess and that is the reason she went overseas!

– 7 –

Mum's Family

While writing this memoir it began to bother me that I had so little knowledge about my family. I knew who my father's parents were, and my aunts and uncles from both sides, but mother's ancestry was a mystery. An unyielding and unspoken family secret seemed to surround that side of the family. It is for this reason that I have given this a separate chapter.

When we were young, Agnes Bradbury, my maternal grandmother lived in Johannesburg, South Africa, and visited us a couple of times. She had very white curly hair and spoke with an unreal British accent, what people today call 'posh'; but it was ultra 'Posh'! Bearing in mind she was born in the nineteenth-century in an unfashionable county, Yorkshire, I believe now as an adult, that like others in similar circumstances she felt the need and wanted to place herself in a putatively elite class of people so that she would be accepted in the wider world. The accent helped her up the social ladder. This was not unusual among women in particular, and others in general from those times, who had few connections and little money. Indeed, you can read about women of low status throughout history (an example being that remarkable person, Daisy Bates[18]) who put on a lot of airs and graces, simply because they came from working class or lower middle class backgrounds.

Agnes was born a Wilson in 1888 in Huddersfield, Yorkshire. There were five children in the family: Herbert, Minnie, Laura, Agnes and Lucy. My mother told me of visiting Huddersfield after Aunt Minnie died and clearing out her house. Apparently this aunt hoarded things like butter papers, at least five years old, brushes without the bristles, tins and tins of fruit and vegetables long past their use by date, 'maggots and mould and more detritus' she explained. A veritable squirrel! I do not know much more about these Yorkshire relatives of Gran Bradbury's although Herbert and Laura emigrated to South Africa. When my Aunt Romola and I visited York in 1988 we stayed

---

[18] *The Passing of the Aborigines*, Daisy Bates, 1938.

at a B&B outside the city walls. The owner of the B&B had a strong Yorkshire accent. Romola commented that the family (meaning the South African Bradburys), had tried hard to get rid of the Yorkshire vowels and that the African contingent looked down on their cousins from the old country. 'We were the sophisticated ones!' Her remarks did not go unnoticed by me. I began to wonder about this shadowy family.

Grandma Bradbury and me c. 1945

My own children and I knew my mother and Aunt Romola's cousin Fred Nicholls and his second wife, because they lived in Johannesburg when we did (1959-1977). Apparently Fred was a handsome youth who rode a horse and played the trumpet. Fred and his first wife (Laura) had a son called John, who as an adult committed suicide. We never knew Laura or John who was married by the time he killed himself. Pat Nicholls, Fred's second wife and he had one son from the marriage, Robert. Fred was besotted with Robert, whatever the boy wanted he got. At one stage Robert was interested in gem polishing. Fred got him a tumbling machine and when they moved from

Bryanston, the house in Parktown had a room devoted to Robert's hobby. Fred took a great interest in and learned all there was to know about cutting, polishing and setting precious and semi-precious stones. Later, when Robert was a teenager, he took up weight lifting, became very muscular, blonded his hair, wore large vulgar rings and was generally a complete philistine. This time the house was filled with numerous pictures of body builders, Fred spoke endlessly about biceps, triceps and 'championships'. Robert was always taciturn and said little about anything and merely grunted when spoken to. Truth was I found Robert an enigma. He and Fred slept in the same room for all of his childhood and teenage; 'A very unhealthy relationship', opined both Aunt Romola and Mum and furthermore, 'Fred took Robert away from his mother'. Meanwhile Pat (Nicholls) kept body and soul together by typing, as a 'temp' in Johannesburg city, playing bridge and tennis and waiting for her substantial inheritance. This waiting period caused the pair of them to behave as if they were penniless and that their solicitors would, 'take it all from us in fees'. One day, Robert too committed suicide. It is believed he was in debt.

Aunt Romola aged 21 years   *Patricia Bradbury aged 21 years*

Their life was not happy.

Early in 2003, right in the middle of writing this memoir, I started asking questions about the maternal side of the family and faxed my Aunt Romola in Port Elizabeth, South Africa asking her what she knew about the Bradburys. She replied that there was nothing she could tell me about the family. I pressed her a bit, telling her I had heard vague stories of a half-sister of theirs called 'Kitty' who lived in Johannesburg and whom they never saw. I had heard about Kitty from the very same Pat Nicholls, though she never elaborated. So my Aunt, bless her heart, decided to tell me what she knew about her and my mother's side of the family. (Apparently Kitty was an 'Aunt' of theirs).

Their father was Samuel Bradbury. For years Romola tried to find out about him through the normal channels. It is believed he was born in Oldham, UK in 1856 – the Chinese year of the Dragon. Knowing what I now know of Samuel, this fits in with the pattern of his whole life. Romola sent me a letter and a marriage certificate and her fax is worth quoting in part:

Sorry about the glitch in my fax. As far as Aunt Kitty was concerned all I know is that she came from Australia. My father had sheep farms there [I wonder where?][19] and he said he had adopted her as she was the daughter of a friend of his. There was also Aunt Betty who was supposed to be her sister. Both ladies married wealthy Johannesburg men and mixed in the highest society. Kitty married James Butler who owned race horses. Betty married Goldly of Goldly, Panchard and Webber. When Goldly died she married Webber.

Aunt Kitty was presented at court she was always resented by my mother. She always said that Kitty should have had Pat – your Mum – presented at court – she could have done so, but didn't. I always felt that my mother turned us against Kitty, which I now regret – because I think she was a nice lady but Mum was eaten up with jealousy, not surprising because Kitty had everything and Mum had nothing.

Agnes Wilson was born in 1888 in Huddersfield, Yorks, and eloped with my father who was, it was believed, married to another woman and

---

[19] Author's query.

may or may not have been divorced. They married in London. He was 28 years older than she was and her parents would not give consent to their marriage. He had a son by a previous marriage, but I never knew him.

The marriage certificate between Agnes Wilson (31) and Samuel William Bradbury (57) was solemnised at the General Registry Office in Lambeth in the County of London on 12 April 1911 in the presence of several male witnesses, but unfortunately the writing is not entirely legible. My Aunt Romola obtained this copy on 21 August 1981.

In a second fax she said:

Having been persuaded by Laura in 1911 or 1912, my parents left England and came out to South Africa and settled in Johannesburg. Samuel was an engineer and the family had plenty of money and mixed with the rich and famous. We always had white nannies. At some stage they moved out to a small holding - Randburg way. Because of 'business reasons' my Dad moved to the Carlton Hotel where I suppose he lived it up. (The reason for this shift in abode was supposed to be about the river in Craighall Park.) [One wonders if it flooded regularly or not - author's note.]

Three children were born of the union, Gordon, the oldest was born in Kirkheaton, Yorkshire on 31 May 1911, However, Pat [my mother Patricia Agnes Kathleen Bradshaw (formerly Hawkey nee Bradbury)] and I (Romola McWilliams [(formerly Fyvie born Bradbury]) were born in Johannesburg. Gordon went to Jeppe High School and left school at 14.[20] He became an assayer at Geldenhuys Deep in Johannesburg, part of Rand Leases. Gordon died at age 45 from an enlarged heart from smoking.

One day in a fit of pique, Mother packed the three children into a trap and all turned up at the hotel to land on my father - I do not know his reaction. At some stage he left for England 'on business' and never returned. He left his money to another woman and the 'farm' to my mother which she sold for a pittance as she needed the money. She

---

[20] Pat and Romola went to Barnato Park Girls High, Johannesburg.

moved to Florida (Transvaal) where my Aunt Laura lived and she became a dress maker to make ends meet. She had a hard life.

It is believed Samuel died in London and was buried at Oak Street Cemetery, (Richmond?)

As a child I'd hear the grown-ups' scrappy conversation about someone called 'Kitty'. My aunt's fax was a revelation to me. Mother probably has knowledge but as she always said and it was her life's credo, 'I never look at the past'.

− 8 −

'She came not but made default'.

One day I found among my personal documents, such as my birth certificate, Dad's marriage certificate to his first wife - a Teresa Sara Catherine Johnstone. The marriage took place at Bulawayo in the Parish of St John the Baptist in the district of Matabeleland on 23 December 1933, after three Banns. Dad's occupation was given as a magistrate's clerk. Her profession: a secretary who lived at the YWCA Hostel Bulawayo. I had lived there too when I was 17 years-old, but father - everyone called him Ted - never told me about her existence. I often wonder what came into his mind when he came to visit me at the YWCA, invariably in something red and sporty. By that time he had 'gone off the rails'.

The divorce certificate that dissolved Teresa and Ted's marriage is quaintly worded - for the defendant in the suit (Teresa):

having been duly summoned to answer John Edward (Plaintiff) in the said [action], came not but made default both at the first hearing on 27 April 1936 and on 27 July 1936 .

I heard of Teresa's existence many years later, apparently Ted did not want us to know he had been married before, and told Mum her name was Tess Hawkins. I never bothered to find out more about Teresa, which I regret, for she was the first of Dad's four wives.

Then I obtained his birth certificate from Somerset House in London. It is on yellow paper with red printing and parts are shaded in faintly lined pink. The seal - General Register Office, England, with an English Coat of Arms - which consisted of the crowned lion, and a unicorn rampant on either side of an heraldic shield with a large crown atop. The seal is raised and is very clear but I cannot make out the design on the shield, even when using my magnifying mirror.

Ted was born John Edward on 11 February 1909 at Tower Road, Newquay to John Wesley Hawkey and Ellen Jane, formerly Goldsworthy. My grandfather's occupation was listed as a builder, she, a housewife of Tower Road, so I realise that Dad was born at home. I, on the other hand, was born at the Lady Dudley Nursing Home in Salisbury on 18 June 1939, (or so I thought). I could have sworn that is what I had been told otherwise how could I know about the Lady Dudley? In fact my birth registered in the District of Salisbury, Rhodesia, states that the Chalaric Nursing Home was the place. Perhaps it was my brother who could lay claim to the Dudley. On my certificate Dad is described as a European from England and Mother, a European from the Transvaal. (Transvaal? Where in the Transvaal?) Actually she was born in Johannesburg, Transvaal, South Africa. Their address is given as 145 Rhodes Avenue, Salisbury. This Certificate has the name Rhodesia printed under the coat of arms – a wildebeest, I think, rampant on either side of a shield bearing an anvil and on top is the famous soapstone bird which had been found by the European explorers in the Zimbabwe Ruins as we knew it then, in Fort Victoria[21]. Generations of explorers insisted that Africans were not capable of such endeavours and believed the ruins had been built by Arab traders or other exotic people and that was the received belief in the West when I was a child. It is only latterly that it has been acknowledged that the Shona tribe had built it. The history of the Zimbabwe Monuments is a study on its own.

There are many other documents in the pile, fragments of my former life. I had need of them when I wanted to lay claim to my British inheritance and give up the Rhodesian passport at the time Ian Smith took a unilateral declaration of independence from Britain in 1965. There are also documents I needed when migrating to Australia, but that is another story.

I was christened Romola Valmai Hawkey – Romola was my mother's sister's name and Valmai my mother's sister-in-law's name. Few people can pronounce them. Romola is *Rom-a-la*, three syllables with emphasis on none of them. It is an Italian name, and the title of a book by George Eliot *Romola*. The dancer Njinsky's wife's was called Romola too so it could have Russian origins. In 2003 we saw on ABC television *Daniel Deronda* where the

---

[21] Masvingo. The Zimbabwe Ruins are now called Zimbabwe monuments.

heroine's name (her real name) is Romola. I have never met another Romola apart from my aunt. As for Valmai, it is Welsh. It is not pronounced Valmay or Valma but Valmi, with an accent on the 'I'. My father had wanted to call me Ingeborg – a Danish name I am told, and so I was called Borgie (with a hard g) as a residue of the name Dad wanted for me. When I was young I loathed the name Romola and so Borgie stuck. This in turn was shortened to Borgs and I was called by this name, or variations of it until I was 18 years-old, at which time I decided it was terrible to be 'Bawgee Hawkey', I wanted something more elegant, in keeping with my grown-up self and so insisted I be called Val, which I am to this day. (Only my brother still calls me Borgs).

Watch That Accent and Mind Your Manners

'Don't say "them"', Dad insisted, 'It's "thim", as in "I asked thim to stay"'. I could not for the life of me get this right, the difference between 'them' and 'thim'. What was Dad getting at? He was very fussy about the way we spoke. I realise he wanted to keep the South African Afrikaans influence from over the border out of our speech. 'Wear, not weh – chair not cheh, et not ate', the list went on. All our elocution lessons came from Dad, as did etiquette, and he was a martinet in this regard.

I was in a play, *The Frog Prince,* and was the Princess. The Prince was one Ricky Aronowitz, with whom I used to physically fight, surprisingly, much to Dad's delight. My father told all and sundry that on the night of the performance when the Princess, i.e. me said: 'I'll give you the beautiful comb that I wear'. Ricky's response was, 'How can I use it without any heh?' This said at ack-ack machine gun rapidity. Dad was appalled. John's take is that Dad had a Rhodesian accent, I do not know if he saw it like that. I suppose he was not unusual as we all have our pet hates, and he had several!

Dad also insisted we use our cutlery properly. 'You don't hold your knife like a pen and on no account are to lay your cutlery off the side of the plate'.

He also wanted us to place our eating utensils together, handles facing the eater when we had finished our meal. 'On no account are you to eat off your knife', or, 'Drink your soup from the side of the soup spoon, and please, no slurping'.

'Borgs, when I introduce you to someone, you must say how-do-you-do, not 'pleezed-ta-meechya', and shake hands. Also remember, if a lady comes to the house you are to show her where the toilet and bathroom are'.

In these aspects of our upbringing Dad was strict. No eating peas from the scoop of our forks, a stupid rule if ever there was, no talking with our mouths full of food. Was his sternness a bad thing? I think not when one sees the way in which young children run wild in an era of 'new parenting', it may be new but not necessarily better.

Who was Dad?

'Can we do a little experiment?' asked Margaret, a psychotherapist I visited in 1993. I was too depressed to refuse. I listened to the gentle soughing of the plane trees and watched the leaves fall for it was a crisp autumn day in her North Sydney consulting rooms, and as it turned out, a very special day at that.

'I want you to sit very quietly and just listen to me', she said bringing me out of my thoughts; 'lay your head on the back of the chair, close your eyes and relax'. I complied. After about five minutes this is what she said I should do.

'Imagine you are in the country, any piece of country anywhere. I want you to observe your surroundings. Look at the trees, grass, the view. Now you will notice you're on a path – at the foothills of a mountain. You wander along this path, it is an easy walk, for although the path is ascending it is on the outer edge of the mountain'. I was following her in my mind's eye. 'The path ascends curving gently upwards, so there is no strain. All the time you should look at the scenery, smell the trees, hear the birds'. (I swear I could smell eucalyptus, see the thorn trees and the msasas. Birds fluttered and sang.) 'After about ten minutes you are almost at the summit, and the path widens, do you see there is a seat up there?' (Yes, I could imagine it to be a brown straight-backed garden seat.) 'At the same time from the summit comes another, wearing something white and concealing', she went on. 'You sit and wait. The person approaches you. Now tell me who is it, Val?'

A sense of shock went through me.

'Oh yes I know who it is'. It was completely clear to me in that second. 'It is my father'.

Dad – John Edwards (Ted) Hawkey, at palm tree c. 1937

'Well', said Margaret placidly, 'Your father sits down and you converse. What is it you are saying?'

'Daddy I am so sorry, so terribly sorry for all that happened. I never said goodbye to you and that is what I want to do now'. All the wretched feelings poured out at that moment. I felt as though I were a child all over again. He smiled, the gentle smile of long ago, of the young man he was years before the breakdown in our relationship. I do not remember much more of what I said to my father then or what he said to me, if anything, but I came away with a great sense of peace, something was closed, finished at last. I suppose the whole thing took twenty minutes.

How did I know that my father and I conversed in this manner? I have no recollection of what Dad looked like on the mountain, apart from his smile, in this most every-day and down-to-earth 'vision' – I was completely conscious.

I was and am deeply curious about this episode in my life, because as anyone can tell you, I am the deepest skeptic of all things mysterious, any jiggery-pokery, past life reincarnations, astrological forecasts etc. I am definitely a contender for the Skeptics Club. Was it Shakespeare who said: 'There are more things in heaven and earth, Horatio, Than are dreamt of in your philosophy?' I think about Dad and I am no longer sad, that psychological meeting on the mountain made me realise I had carried grief for him for a long time which is now resolved. But the burning question remains, how did it happen?

•

Who then was this person, John Edward (Ted) Hawkey who fathered me? When you are young things happen, statements are made, you have so little understanding of other people, or their motives, and that things that happen may not be regarded as normal. This is especially true of parents who are all-powerful and who play to a captive audience – their children. I remember that Dad was very kind to both of us when we were young, and I longed to hear from him that I was his favourite child. I nagged him over and over 'Am I your favourite, Dad?' He would reply, 'You are my favourite daughter'. Somehow this never satisfied me. The psychology of all this of course was the difficult relationship I had with Mum. Later I could see things I never knew then, about Dad and Mum who brought their baggage and their secrets into the union. I believe, according to my Aunt Valmai, that Mum had once been engaged to an Ernest Bodley and when he broke it off she visited Rhodesia, met Dad and married on the rebound – and Dad? We will never know; he was an enigma. I knew his parents who were straight-forward and rather narrow, and his Aunt and Uncle. But Dad was an unknown quantity. He seemed to love my mother but even as a child I realised she had colourless feelings for him. He was very affectionate to all of us and Mum was not. Such different psyches I feel are bound to bring turmoil in their interaction with each other.

We are young. Dad is a happy, loving father. He plays 'grizzly bears' which reduces us to screams of mock terror. When he comes home we shout in anticipation, 'Dad, Daddy, play bears with us'. Much growling and chasing ensues. He is musical too and plays the ukulele; his favourite song is, we think, aptly named 'He Played his Ukulele When the Ship Went Down'; (when I was much older I found out it was called 'The Wreck of the Nancy Lee'), the lyrics of which intrigue me, as the protagonist being shipwrecked is heard singing and playing the uke. Did he reach the bottom of the ocean? I could imagine the swirling depths, the starfish, the seaweed and a man looking like a shipwrecked sailor with pigtail, cut off pants and striped socks playing away merrily on his ukelele. I got the image from the illustrations of one of my books. We like 'Don't Fence Me In'. Another favourite on the uke is 'Two Little Girls in Blue, Lad'. (I think it's called 'Two Little Girls in Blueland'). The tune is jolly but I know the content is sad. Also a song which makes me sad and nostalgic is one he particularly likes called 'Early One Morning'. I imagine the poor maiden in the valley below – so badly treated with garlands in her hair, it is all so vivid.

Dad entertains us some evenings at home, sitting in the lounge singing all these tunes and strumming away. He is charming and we love every minute of his playing. But later he stops playing his ukelele as the domestic scene changes and Dad with it.

We have two lots of friends who live across the railway line, a Greek family called Venturas with a daughter called Phoebe, and the Moffats. Moffat is a name associated with Dr Robert Moffat, who explored Rhodesia and in 1857, persuaded Mzilikazi to set up a mission station at Anita. It was Moffat who alleviated the King's chronic medical condition of dropsy (Lobengula?) '...due to a diet of quantities of beef washed down by pot after pot of Kaffir beer'.[22] Whether our Que Que Moffats were related to Dr Robert I do not know. There are three young boys in the family, their father a lawyer, and there is something funny, a secret attaches to Mrs Moffat, as we never see her, but sometimes are aware that she is in a bedroom in the house. The Moffats have a fine collection of 'cowboy songs', (we have never heard of the expression 'Country and Western'). Roy Rogers and Gene Autry we love.

---

[22] Robert Blake, *A History of Rhodesia*. London: Methuen, 1977, p.22.

One memorable day our father comes with us to the Moffats and plays their records for us (being Dad, John the two Moffat boys and me). The Moffat seniors are not at home. One record we play I think at that time is called 'Change Back to Old Virginny, Back to My Clicks Mountain Home'. Then there's 'Take me Back to my Boots and Saddle', 'I'm an Old Cowhand from the Rio Grande' and 'A Four Legged Friend'. We play them over and over. We just steep ourselves in that music on a magic day. Afterwards we wander around their garden which is filled with trees, fruit and flower beds meticulously marked out and sectioned off. There are the ubiquitous gravel paths, the red poinsettias and purple Morning Glory running riot over a pergola. Stables for two horses are at the back and the property edges the town. The house has a long mosquito netted veranda and is made of stone, but apart from the record room we are never invited into the house, which, from the outside looking through the windows appears to be pitch black. Perhaps the curtains are drawn. Somehow I never remember another day when our father is so close to us.

Years later Mother tells me that Mrs Moffat was an alcoholic and was sent away for rehabilitation, and that 'poor man met her on the station, and she staggered off the train drunk'. She also told me that from time to time Mrs Moffat came knocking on our front door asking for liquor. Alcoholism in Rhodesia was probably rife, one withdraws from mentioning it even today – then it was closeted, no-one dared speak its name. To have an alcoholic mother was taboo.

•

However, there are some unpleasant aspects of life with Dad. He likes shooting game and often takes us with him, especially after the rains. It delights us to accompany him. He loads the car with his .22 rifle. I never like the shooting, but want to stay in Dad's good books and keep up with my brother who is so good at spotting wild animals. I am hopeless because I secretly hate it when we find one and I see them falling hopelessly from a bullet and to watch them in their death throes, their beautiful eyes glazing over. We are driven north of Que Que, rather slowly, and John and I are supposed to peer through the tall camouflage of trees and long grass to find the tell-tale horns of buck. When something is seen, invariably by my brother, he shouts, 'Dad. Dad. I've spotted something!' He is so accurate at finding animals, he never fails in his mission. Sure enough, there in the shade of the Mopani trees is a family of buck.

'Good boy', says Dad with great conviction, 'You've got wonderful eyesight'. And indeed my brother keeps his 20/20 vision right into his sixties. Meanwhile, Dad quietly leaves the car, aims the gun usually from over the back wheel area. There is a great stillness punctuated with a sharp 'crack', which reverberates and echoes, causing the leaves of the trees to shake and a great twittering and birds to flutter away. The poor beast is felled. Dad seems indifferent, callous and rather ruthless on these particular days (which are marked out by the shootings).

Occasionally the shooting expedition lasts a whole weekend, which obviously entails camping. Dad brings along a native whom he finds, heaven knows where. This person packs the car; the gray-green tent unearthed from the garage, sleeping bags, and a few pots and pans, kerosene lamp and a small stove. All are taken along for the expedition. Our helper rigs the tent, fastens the guy ropes, sets out the sleeping bags, crockery and cutlery then helps skin and gut the kill. Some of the game is eaten at the camp-site but mostly the carcasses are brought home to be cooked by Campbell for our dinner, or Dad gives them to his friends. Our mother never accompanies us and I do not believe that I have any idea of her views on the matter. Today, I do not like to think too much about these shooting sprees, because, people like Dad and those that followed after that era when conservation was not considered, helped reduce Rhodesia's wild game to no more than is found in the reserves today. One sees nothing in the bush in the third millennium and Zimbabwe is the poorer for it.

Dad loves music. He is not highbrow in his taste, though he listens to opera occasionally with Mother – 'Your Tiny Hand is Frozen' – Benjamino Gigli with his passionate and heroic voice ringing out, being her favourite. Rather, my father likes the popular tunes from America and buys records for his new 78rpm record player with needles that require changing when blunt. This was before the portable gramophone and the diamond stylus. Gershwin's 'Rhapsody in Blue' and the Inkspots singing 'Bless you for Being an Angel' and 'Whispering Grass' are among his favourites. He particularly likes the Ink Spots. Other songs that Dad fancies are 'Deep Purple' and 'Stormy Weather' all the rage in Rhodesia then. Anything by Bing Crosby, from 'Don't Fence Me In', 'White Christmas' to 'We'll Make Love when it Rains', Dad loves them all. I like 'Too Young' by Nat King Cole, so Dad purchases that for me. Its melancholic tune resonates somewhere in my young heart. Dad has an endless tune whirling through his brain and whistles, mostly between his teeth, everywhere he goes. We siblings also have the habit. I find it strange to hear John's tuneless whistle which emulates Dad, of which he is probably quite unconscious.

One morning, while sitting on a bench in the Westfield Shopping Centre, in Chatswood, New South Wales, with a mass of people wandering around, right outside the Ooh!! La! La! jewellery shop, sometime in the late 1980s, I heard an Ink Spots song playing over the shopping centre Tannoy. I sat there and cried. This was before my visit to Margaret the psychologist.

•

Although my family's musical in that they love music and Dad plays an instrument, we know nothing of African music which is strange, especially in view of the explosion of African music now available and popular. In fact my parents whose views probably are those of the wider community in Southern Rhodesia, find African music primitive and their dancing abhorrent. We know nothing about people like the guitar picker of the late 40s and early 50s, George Sibanda, even though he came from Bulawayo!

I never see African dancing until I visit the Simmer and Jack mine in Johannesburg years later where we are entertained by many African groups, particularly the Zulus and their gumboot dancing. Their rhythm is electrifying, they leap about slapping their gumboots and singing. Gumboot dancing becomes my favourite type of African dancing.

Dad is obsessed with clean shoes. Today, he would be diagnosed as having a form of obsessive compulsive disorder, because when he is wandering Rhodesia after his demise as a magistrate, he books himself into a hotel, and bring dozens of pairs of shoes with him. On one occasion I visit him at a hotel in Bulawayo and find him surrounded by rows and rows of smart expensive shoes which he had laid out on the floor. While polishing and buffing them he whistles endlessly. He believes a person should always keep up their sartorial appearances. Good shoes and clothing mark someone out as special and prosperous. He also leaves things behind wherever he goes, glasses, gloves, umbrellas, cigarette lighters, cigarettes, cigarette cases all gone – another failing I inherit.

Every morning after his bath, Dad Brylcreems his black curly hair which he wears swept back flat against his scalp. The Brylcreem turns the curls into tight waves. I see my father with a towel draped around his waist, black curly chest hair; both the slicked black hair and hairy chest so very unfashionable today when smooth bodies are favoured. In his later years he resembles Richard Nixon, with the same receding hair line, vertically seamed cheeks, but without the ski-jump nose. He always wears a suit and tie, his dress impeccable. His shoes, as mentioned earlier, polished by Richard are left outside the bedroom door for Dad to step into once he had risen.

Dad's day-to-day existence consists of going to His (and after 1953), Her Majesty's Magistrate's Court to work, where he deals mainly with Africans who have legal infringements. The road is lined with silky oaks, their pretty honey-coloured flowers shine in the sun like fish vertebrae, the leaves gracefully and lazily wave in the breeze. The ever-present guards are at the front door, and when they see Dad arriving up the gravel path they salute him; hands to brimmed hats, heels in their black boots sharply brought together. There is a wire fence around the property and large shady trees, mostly jacarandas. Dad's bench is a highly polished wooden desk, and the seating in the court house green leather, rather like the leather on the Rhodesia Railways, with wooden trim. Ceiling fans cool the air; the windows open outwards, none of the sealed hermetic atmosphere experienced today. I do not go to 'Dad's court' often, and never when court is in session, but remember visiting on Sundays if Dad wants to pick something up. I do not know for sure, but think he is a good magistrate though one could not say that he works hard. In retrospect he seems unmotivated, filled with a sense of *ennui*. He once wrote a book about his time on the bench, but the manuscript was never published and has disappeared today. His insights would have helped in writing this memoir.

He does not play any sport, but has an abiding love for photography. He particularly likes Leica cameras, I can see in my mind's eye the Leica logo. It is a name I have never forgotten. Dad buys all the photography magazines available in those days. One is called *Aperture*. His specialty is taking pictures of cloud formations and roads in the country that go off into the horizon. He also takes many photos of all of us. He turns our spare bedroom, the one that leads onto the veranda, into a dark room, and sometimes I spend time there with him. It is rather spooky, with the blue indigo light and the pans of liquid into which he places his films, but the results are pretty impressive. He has an excellent eye for form and light, all the photos are in black and white where contrast matters. We have packets and packets of photos, spilling everywhere, an endless supply of pictures of cumulus clouds, trees, roads, some of the family and friends; there are so many that in the end they become a mere utility we do not appreciate: a pity, mainly because like our lives the photos have dispersed and drifted away. A pity also because Dad had a distinct talent. Only two landscapes survive. One is of a magnificent rumble of clouds, the other, an unnamed Zimbabwean river, as smooth as glass, with reflections of the shoreline. They are unmistakably my father's photos.

Dad is not a fall-down drunk, he does not slur his words and never stumbles when walking, or at least I never saw him do this, but alcohol has the most profound effect on him resulting in a complete personality change. His parents, long deceased, were, as I mentioned earlier, temperance folk, and when they visit us, which is rarely, Dad insists that every single bottle top, bottles and all paraphernalia to do with the drinking of liquor be thrown out or hidden away. He couldn't bear the fact that his parents would cotton on to his great destructive secret. This obsession and guilt about his drinking runs deep.

Watching my father teaches me a lot about alcoholics, which stands me in good stead, an essential knowledge for life. When a lot younger and still living in Que Que, Dad goes drinking at the Globe and Phoenix Club most nights after work. Mum's dinners are ruined, there are rows, after which he went through bouts of remorse where he was 'never going to drink again, ever'.

Sometime in the early 1950s Dad's behaviour becomes odd, he develops facial tics, and the paranoia that is to plague him begins to surface. People avoid him. He tries extra hard to get on side with us. He tells everyone who'll listen to him how his children 'are everything in the world to me'. In later years, when we live with him in Fort Victoria he uses manipulative verbal abuse, and whenever things go wrong he goes on and on about the incident in question, all this in a low rumble, almost a mutter, over and over in a manner I find completely overwhelming. This has a deeply traumatic effect. In relation to this, I remember reading an Agatha Christie who-dunnit which Mum also reads.

'The character in this book is exactly like your father', she says. 'Using emotional blackmail to reduce everyone to a latent terror'.

Dad relates endless anecdotes about people who like and admire him. Some write him letters thanking him for what he has done, though he never reads these, (if indeed they exist), to us. There is also a marked tendency to believe he is a martyr to the ironies of fate. Nothing he does is ever his fault and he does not admit to his alcoholism. At this time he smokes endlessly, a black filter gripped between his teeth, while he regales us all. Dad eats nothing at this stage in his life. His teeth are stained, and he has the yellow hue of nicotine on the first two fingers of his right hand. Then, he becomes ill and visits the local doctor who informs him he has the early stages of scurvy. How could anyone in the twentieth-century get to that state, you may well ask!

•

When I leave school, early in 1957, I move to the YWCA in Bulawayo. I have been living with Mum and Tony for some years prior to this. Dad who is suspicious of everyone and everything and finds fault with all and sundry, starts visiting the YWCA, ostensibly to see me. He approaches my teenage girlfriends asking them out, particularly the beautiful Danish girl Gita Westlarsen with her long blond hair and legs that went on forever, and is furious when rebuffed, saying all my friends are 'gauche and unsophisticated'. My friends and I are *so* embarrassed, and we all dread his unannounced visits, once in a natty red sports car which he crashes a few weeks after purchasing it. Dad is by now decidedly odd and I suspect he was trying to impress, this is a comical moment!

Stories do the rounds about his manipulative behaviour, how he shows unwanted interest in my widowed Aunt Valmai living in Gwelo, his fights and car crashes. Dad fancies the opposite sex and believes they are attracted to him. One story of his exploits is, while pursuing a woman who lived in Bulawayo, he came banging on her door one night at about midnight, no doubt drunk as the proverbial Lord. She tells him to go away. He then knocks up the person living next door and somehow persuades him (for it was a man) to let him in so that he, Ted, could climb out of the man's window onto the ledge under her window and thereby get into the flat of the woman he was chasing. She is livid and as you can imagine the relationship faltered.

He claims that one night he and his African companion see a flying saucer outside Fort Victoria. People ask what pub he visited! Perhaps he did see something, but as a witness to events, his evidence is regarded as not credible so we will never know. He has little or no insight into his failings and his illness.

At some stage, I am not sure when, because a chronology of events becomes a casualty when discussing the whens and wheres of my father's life, he joined Alcoholics Anonymous and although he never recovered his old personality, he got off the drink. That however, was not the end, for unbeknownst to me he had what was a long time substitute. It was his great friend Bill Payne, a tall, loose-limbed man with a typical pale northern hemisphere complexion and reddish hair, who told me about Dad's addiction. I had found a shoe-box full of small bottles of tablets, about forty of them.

This was not in Que Que but while on a school vacation, visiting a couple who were friends of Dad's (he was staying with them at the time and was supposed to be entertaining me, but had buzzed off somewhere). These people lived in a small mining town. I do not know where or how Dad knew them. I asked Bill what the tablets were and he told me Dad was hooked on Benzedrine, Ephedrine and Dexedrine, classic uppers and downers. I was shocked. Who provided them? Obviously Dad had a compliant and obliging doctor or chemist. But where? The amphetamines exacerbated Dad's problem. He started taking them after he had joined AA, or so I thought, but I later learnt from Mum he was on them when we lived in Que Que. She told me that one day she saw the 'boy' from the local chemist riding his bike. When he espied Mum he braked and took a brown envelope out of his saddle bag. 'Please will madam give this to the boss?' He handed her an account rendered. Naturally, Mum looked at it. The balance due was a sizable amount. Dad was buying 1,500 tablets a month! In those days no-one knew how addictive amphetamines were.

Sometime after the amphetamine affair, I remember being called to a hospital by my grandparents whom I never saw at this stage in my life. I was still at boarding school and I think it was the Bulawayo hospital. There was Dad, lying on the bed, swearing at the nurses, angry and unpleasant. His parents were utterly dumbfounded and dreadfully upset. They had never known about Dad's problems and facing the awful truth so late in their lives was most disquieting for them.

'I never knew that Edward swore', said Gran, her eyes filled with tears, 'Or that he was drinking'.

Don't talk to me about it, I thought – I do not want to know. I wanted to run away and so put this incident and my poor grandparents out of my mind. I was about 17 years-old at the time. I never contacted or saw them again which I regret.

Twenty-five years after Dad had committed suicide in the Princess Margaret Hospital in Salisbury (1960), one morning while drinking coffee in Bundanoon, New South Wales, I had the first and only conversation with my brother about our mother and father and his life with Dad after the family's disintegration. John told me an anecdote about Dad and his drinking. The story goes that John and Dad and local police from one of the towns where they were living at that time went shooting game. After a day's shooting the adults began serious drinking. Then horror, the alcohol ran out! They were miles from anywhere and it was the middle of the night. According to a witness, 'Ted was beside himself. We all realised that for him to have no liquor was an absolute death sentence. He was in a blue funk of panic'.

After my parents were divorced John went to Christian Brothers College in Sea Point in the Cape Province of South Africa. Dad had custody of John who 'lived' with Dad and in his school holidays. Dad would hit the road, taking John to every pub in every town throughout Rhodesia. There were times when the two of them were ostensibly domiciled in South Africa, mostly in Cape Town, for Dad was always on the move running away from his demons. It was where he met his fourth wife. I believe she was a red haired Afrikaans woman called Rita whom I never met.

Reading over this potted history of my father I realise that I had loved him dearly when I was little and felt that I was somehow to blame because I could not save him from himself. Later, when I was older, he was a great disappointment to me and I was angry with him for years, all that waste and destruction. However, after I visited him in the psychiatric wing of the Princess Margaret Hospital in Salisbury, I saw him as a frail, rather sad figure, definitely on the edge of madness and the negative attitude towards him disappeared. Shortly after this visit Dad hanged himself on the bell-cord above his bed. His psychiatrist told me that the hospital had given him shock treatment which seemed initially to pep him up. However, within a few days he was talking about how the CID in Rhodesia was out to get him. He wandered around the ward, looking wild eyed and saying, 'There is only one crime they cannot get you for', alluding of course to suicide, although no-one knew his true intention at the time. The psychiatrist went on to say that the shock treatment had, in a manner of speaking, blown away all the leaves of his depression revealing his deep paranoia.

John always said: 'Dad was a very nice man', and probably he was – at his core.

PART TWO

The Residency, Fort Victoria, 1999

—9—

The Convent

IT is Sunday, the Angelus' doleful notes are the first thing I hear. I'm not dreaming, on the contrary, this is the hated Bulawayo Convent, my nadir, repressive and overwhelming. How did I land up here? I am 11 years-old, going on 12 and no-one consulted me or spoke to me about coming to this place.

Sunday is by far the worst day of the week at the Convent. At no time is this more apparent than those awful breakfasts in the dining room at the eastern point of the Convent. The sunlight glittered palely on the white napery. On every table stands a large urn of water for tea. We'd sit down with a scraping of chairs.

'Time for Grace'.

Heads down, hands folded.

'For what we are about to receive may the Lord make us *truly* grateful. Ay-men'

Vienna sausages and white bread, washed down with tea, that's our Sunday fare. An awful combination. The smell of hot Viennas, bursting red skins, the aroma of tea, the girls' muddy shoes and the pale, white, margarined bread; everything a precursor to the utterly excruciatingly boring remaining hours of the Sabbath. I feel impotent, isolated, helpless as only a young child can be, and am filled with anxiety at my abandonment.

The Catholics among us go to mass early on Sundays. They talk amongst themselves about it.

'I got indulgences, look at my Holy Cards'.

'Today, I went to confession. Do you know if you lie that's a venal sin?'

'Are you baptized?' This question addressed to me.

I shake my head, because I do not know whether I am baptized or not.

'Ooh! You'll go to limbo when you die'. This said in a conspiratorial whisper. Brown and blue eyes look at me pityingly.

Those of us who are not of the faith go on dreary crocodile walks: twenty or so little girls dressed in our Sunday best, hats, white socks and highly polished shoes – we shuffle along. The nun in front, eyes downcast.

'Don't you girls look at the boys!'

Would the horror never end! Every aspect of our lives is tightly controlled. It is my punishment, but for what I do not know.

•

It is Christmastime when I discover I am being sent at the beginning of the following year to a convent, the Bulawayo Convent, as a boarder. I am told I am going there for multiple reasons.

'You'll do well at that school', says Dad, 'The nuns are *born* teachers'. (I think about what Dad says and wonder how you are born a teacher. I knew born referred to babies, so it is a puzzle I can't work through).

'Yes, the nuns are noted for their, um! for their attention to scholarly achievement'. This is Mum. 'Besides, it will do you good'. Meaning Mum would get me away from 'unsuitable friends'.

'But I want to stay at Que Que School', I start whining.

They do not voice the real and underlying reason – the breakdown of a tenuous relationship between the pair, and Mum's inability to cope with the stresses of our lives. She and Ted are fighting constantly, either about 'burnt dinners or hours waiting alone'. Sometimes it's about 'bar-fly friends', a litany of complaints. Dad starts calling her 'Homer'. 'You're always saying you want to go home just when the party is starting'. I hear all this growling and grumbling while lying in bed at night.

At some stage a clothing list arrives itemising socks, underwear, shoes, uniforms, blazer. I do not remember how many items there were, but there are clothes for summer and winter and expensive leather shoes, brown.

'Goodness, they cost a lot', and this, according to Mum, is 'quite outrageous'.

Mum takes sew-on tapes from her sewing drawer. She marks the tapes to go onto the new outfits with an indelible pen: *Romola Hawkey* Meanwhile Esther sits there, her mouth full of pins, sewing them into the neckbands or waists of my new clothes, and she throws the finished ones onto a small mound ready for packing.

I assume a timetable and outline of the convent's mission was sent as well. I wonder when and how all the inquiries about the convent came about, how many letters or telephone calls did it take in preparation for my exile. I dimly

THE GUINEA FOWL GIRL

realise this is my fate, and watch them packing all the expensive school clothing with dread, ticking off the items on a list as they do so.

'Three white shirts, six pairs of white pants, six hankies, four vests, Oh dear, we've missed sewing tapes into some of these socks'. The pen poised irresolutely over the list.

'Esther, please put tapes into that pair over there. I'll continue....blazer, hat, hat band'.

No matter what Mum and Dad say about being sent to boarding school, I do not fancy it, especially as no-one tells me *exactly* why I am going. They just make a lot of excuses. It is all a terrible shock and I am full of apprehension. And so the day arrives. I leave my home, the comfort of my own room, the familiarity of the large black-barked tree which I can see outside my window, its soft lethargic leaves gently waving in the morning breeze; the soft early scrape-scrape of the convicts raking the gravel, the muted sounds from the kitchen, breakfast being prepared, my brother's companionship. All the usual things that are part of our domestic life.

'Goodbye Daddy'.

'Goodbye my favourite daughter, now work hard and we will see you in the holidays'.

I kiss Dad; he hugs me close to his comforting body. I whistle tunelessly, holding back the tears. I must have said goodbye to all the servants and to John, because Mum is taking me to Bulawayo on her own.

We motor south and arrive in the city of Bulawayo on a day with the bluest skies, the kind that only Bulawayo can turn on. It's a pretty town, with sandstone buildings, flamboyant trees with their gorgeous red flowers lining the wider than average streets. The streets are designed so that a team of sixteen oxen can make a comfortable and complete turn.[23] Most of the inhabitants have a leisurely life, regulated by the working day of 8am to 4pm for the sun sets early.

However, Bulawayo has a sad history. The word 'Gu-Bulawayo' is the Ndabele for the 'the place of the killing',[24] so named in the time of Mzilikazi. The deaths took place on Thabas Indunas (Hill of Chiefs) which occupies a

---

[23] In June 1994 Bulawayo as a city celebrated its centenary.
[24] Tredgold in *The Rhodesia That Was My Life* describes it as 'the place of the man who was killed', a reference to the civil war with which Lobengula's reign began (p.95).

Rhodes statue, Bulawayo

site close to the town today. The account of 'Gu-Bulawayo' features large in the excellent 1996 biography of Rhodes by Antony Thomas. Lobengula, King of the Matabele, whose encampment was in the area was tricked and out-manoeuvred by Rhodes and his cohorts. Later, realising the game was up, he left his people to Rhodes who was supposed to look after their wellbeing. Outside Bulawayo in the Matopos Hills, a rocky outcrop, is where Cecil John Rhodes is buried. His body lies under a concrete slab, so hardy that African guerillas, under Joshua Nkomo, fighting for their independence from white rule tried to detonate Rhodes from his grave but were not successful in ejecting his corpse.[25] The rest, to invoke the old cliché, is history.

However, this was a forgotten history because the Ndebele loss and despair made no impression on white settlers who dismissed it. When I was young, the word 'Bulawayo' was corrupted and trivialised by Rhodesian teenage boys sitting in the local bars and aspiring to make the largest burp - 'Bullll- a - wayyy oo', usually after imbibing too much beer.

The roads are immaculate, tarred, with solid homes and gardens on either side. We arrive at the convent. It looks enormous to me, looming ominously,

---

[25] A. Thomas, *Rhodes*, 1994 (p.16).

Historical Bulawayo

redly, under those cerulean skies above the stone wall that surrounds it. There are several high-tensile heavy gates with bolts that shut implacably. The buildings have two pointed roof lines and I can see across the vast quadrangle which leads to more buildings at the back. The gray stone Catholic Church abuts the western wall up to the road. Mum takes me to the Mother Superior's office. The room is bright and sunny, painted white, with pleasant furniture. She interviews me briefly, a cold, forbidding woman wearing a silver cross on her breast. She calls me 'Romola'. (Who *is* this Romola person?) When she speaks to Mum, she gives her a glacial and intimidating smile, but no-one intimidates Mum who can metaphorically slay anyone within sight with her dagger-like-dirty looks and cold peremptory tone of voice. I am not listening to what they say to each other but rather taking in the alabaster statue of Mary with her lifeless eyes and the large cross on the wall.

Mum seems happy to say goodbye to me, for she has troubles of her own to deal with back home and no doubt is pleased to have one less with which to contend. With a perfunctory peck on the cheek (Mum never kisses me), and 'Be good and work hard', she's gone. I feel alone and scared.

A girl older than I appears silently at Mother Superior's door.

'This is Romola', she says, 'Please take her to the northern dormitory'.

'Yes, Mother Superior', she bobs. The student looks at me.

'Funny name', she says.

'Oh! I am really Borgie, or Borgs'.

She digests this extraordinary fact rolling her eyes a little from side-to-side. 'Come, er! Baw, Baw'.

'Borgie'.

'OK, Borgie, come with me'.

We go up a green painted iron stairway to the north facing dormitory. She mutters something I can't quite hear to the nun on duty and as silently as she materialised, she disappears.

'Good morning young lady'. Her bleak nun's smile is hardly welcoming. 'I'll show you where you're to sleep'.

The dormitory is an ordinary, long room with about twenty beds, a far cry from my Dolly Varden designed bedroom and the birds that twitter in the morning. Another dormitory separated by the ablution block lies at the southern end. An open space links the dormitories and the ablutions. At night green blinds are lowered to darken the rooms. The convent is run by the Dominicans.[26] We believe they are a German order, because in that year of our Lord 1949, they were a severe bunch and several of them were decidedly Teutonic. The Catholic Church, as the Australian author Thomas Kenneally said in a recent article in *The New Yorker,* 'was a cold and largely self-interested corporate institution'. I receive not a kind word of encouragement and am shown not an iota of affection while there.

The Dominicans wear the wimple, a starched headdress covering their hair and ears which falls in a train below the shoulders. In the front, the neck is encased in what a child would describe as a sort of concertina, so only the face is visible. Black outfits and white aprons, or so I remember. They look to me for all the world like a waddle of penguins, their body shapes uniformly large; all efficiency and starched severity, their gold wedding rings mark them out as Brides of Christ!

I soon realise our collective nemesis is Sister Bibiana (Bibiana the Barbarian), a small dumpy person with a strong German accent who rushes

---

[26] In 1890, Jesuit and Dominican sisters followed Rhodes' settlers. In 1892 the Chishawasha Mission was established close to Salisbury and schools in Salisbury and Bulawayo were erected. These sisters also had training programmes for girls as well as clinics and hospitals.

everywhere, rings bells and yells at the girls. We hate her. But now, I have some sympathy for her in that unhappy set-up. Bibiana is hard-pressed by her charges. I remember another dormitory nun who deals with us too, she has a long brown skinny face, black eyes, her very glance seems to penetrate my soul. I am fascinated by her moles because, before Mum had hers cut out, she too was moley. I don't know this particular nun's name. She is a frigid personality, much quieter than Bibiana, but I feel her presence.

The boarding school of thick sandstone is built to last a millennium, with dormitories overlooking a street lined with droopy-leafed jacarandas, their riotous mauve flowers appearing miraculously every November mocking the controlled life endured in the Convent. Then, the blooms are gone as quickly as they arrived, their spent force lining the pavements with decaying trumpet-shaped flowers. Back home in Que Que, where we too had jacarandas, we put them on our fingers playing ladies with long mauve painted nails.

Every morning at 6am either the Barbarian or the Other One comes in ringing a metal bell with wooden handle.

'Come on you girls, time to get up'.

Yawning and miserable, especially on those cold, wintry Bulawayo mornings when the wind brings fingers of frost, we rise, troop to the communal basins for the usual morning ablutions and down to breakfast.

To exit the dormitories we walk along a corridor, down steps to the ground floor to a large assembly hall on the western end which is in a tower. Upstairs to the left in that tower are the music rooms with their lead-light windows, and in front of the hall an apron-stage for concerts. Everything is built of stone, from the buildings to the paving.

I remember the long-walled passageway with its concrete flooring, which leads from the dormitories on the way to and from the dining room or the school. At the end of the passageway is a large picture of the head of Christ, stuck about with thorns, bleeding. I dread seeing the image. The more I think about it now, the more it becomes a place of sheer misery, words I reiterate to explain that time in the convent.

All of were fascinated by the enclosed garden tucked into the central area bounded by the buildings which delineates the space of the U shape. We imagine the nuns are quartered, you could not stay they 'live' there; 'living' associated with the Catholic assembly is not a concept a 12-year-old can grasp. They are so unbelievable – not real, more like the personification of a nightmare that follows one into the light of morning. The garden has an 8 foot wall which is too high to peer over, so all is supposition. We fantasize constantly, discussing the nuns among ourselves.

'Do they have proper hair under those crinkly things?'

'Wimple, silly'.

'You know they shave their heads!'

'They don't, it's long. They push it underneath the band on their foreheads'.

'Do they wear pants?'

We were certain that not one of them had ever seen a brassiere let alone wear such a contraption.

'What about speaking to each other?'

I think each and every one of them is hideous but keep my disloyalty a secret.

There is much talk among the Catholic girls about 'Father'. I never saw this person whom they revere, but know that he has power or at least authority over the nuns. 'Father' it seems knows everything, he gets his information straight from the Pope and the Pope straight from God. I accept all they say, but understand nothing.

The Convent goes in for gardens and there are several well-cultivated gardens and fruit trees behind the dining room and around the western end: eucalyptus and pepper trees, with the same banded caterpillars they have at the Globe and Phoenix Club in Que Que. Their berries giving off an acrid smell. A tarred quadrangle leads to the double-story classrooms, and you can see the church clearly against the western wall. Occasionally I enter that place, a church filled with bleeding hearts, crosses, sad patient women, a beatified baby, a picture of Jesus with radiant clouds striking his shoulders and hair. Today, I think it is superstitious clap-trap!

Children come from all over the country to board. There are little girls, one as young as six, playing with their rosary beads, clacking away while saying their Hail Marys and getting Holy Cards and seeking indulgences – all are steeped in the ritual of Catholicism. I wonder what happened to them, how warped they must have been with sin and damnation and Satan waiting for any chance to grab the unsuspecting soul. If the children found it all horrible, in those days there was no comforting counsellor to turn to.

Mum, despite the fact she sent me to the convent, in fact both my parents are worried stiff that I might be tainted, by 'religion'. They don't want me to go to Mass but every day I heard all about purgatory, hell and damnation, venal sins, and how little children, unbaptised went limbo. All this from the children!

The nuns are obsessive about bodily impurity which they pass on to us, their charges. They show by their actions what they think about the bits God has given his earthly creation. No child can expose flesh before, during, or after bathing.

'Use your towel'.

So we wrap ourselves in our towels, fearful that we will get bawled at if an inch of breastbone is exposed, or worse, eternal damnation awaits us. What a ridiculous sight, young pubescent or teenage girls wandering around the bathrooms clutching their towels, terrified they might fall off and expose their vulnerable flesh. I find it so appalling and so stressful that at a certain stage I discover how I can avoid bathing for weeks on end and boast about it to my colleagues.

'Hey, I haven't had a bath you know'.

The girls gaze at me, but are not impressed one way or the other. The atmosphere of hatred for the female body permeates our lives, and psychologically we absorb it all.

One morning I fall ill with boils and carbuncles. One of the nuns whom, I imagine was medically trained examines me.

'Hmm! not nice', she says. She ambles off – her white skirts flapping, her black boots squeaking and returns in a little while with plasters which she applies to my throbbing flesh.

'These will draw those boils of yours'.

The plasters are changed daily, but the boils take weeks to clear up. I hasten to add they have nothing to do with my unwashed body. And they reoccur. Perhaps the diet of insufficient greens and fruit exacerbates the problems. Whatever the reason, my skin continues its eruptions. I am moved into a small day-room away from the rest of the students. That makes my stress worse. I live in dread that my mother would die and I will be there forever, abandoned. Depression sets in.

But, by far the worst thing about a school like the convent is the breeding of bullies. Girls, larger and older than I who dislike me, bash me.

'What are you looking at?'

This at prep-time. My heart sinks. The usual scenario will fall into place, I know it.

'Nothing', eyes cast down. It doesn't help. A horrible angry face appears at my side. Bash, fists flew, hair is pulled. I scream and blub. Unbelievably, not a nun, for all their vigilance, sees a thing!

Then come the anxiety attacks, almost every day, though no-one knows about them, and I can't explain them anyway. A feeling of dread assails me, my heart races so fast I think I'll drop dead. Buildings seem menacing, changing shape, looming over me, especially the stone ones of the convent. I feel as if my thoughts are outside my head. At 12 years-old this is very frightening! When Dad visits me I tell him I am 'sick', but don't know how to tell him how exactly I am sick, because when attacks pass the disordered feelings go with them, and memory of the experience too. There are no words in the language to spell out what I feel.

Dad takes me to a children's psychiatrist in Bulawayo, I remember the room and the doctor's white coat. He is a kind man, but I can't describe to him how it is at the time of the attacks. I don't even know I am having 'attacks'. He asks me lots of questions and concludes I am insecure – too true. Like all of us who suffer these attacks, the knowledge that they come unbidden with no warning is the worst aspect. And so it was then. Years later, while living in Sydney, I was at last diagnosed – my malady had a name – panic attacks, anxiety. Oh the joy of naming the unnameable.

Another bizarre aspect of convent life for the juniors is the pressure by other girls to have what they describe as 'a pash (passion) for a senior girl' which gives you the dubious pleasure of making that person's bed and running errands.

'What about so-and-so?' I can't remember the girl upon whom I am to have a supposed 'pash'.

'You have got to make her bed'.

'I don't know how to'. (The black staff made our beds at the convent and at home). 'She's okay, I suppose'.

'Well, go and see her anyway'.

I feel nothing whatsoever for her, and I remember nothing about her, not her name or what she looks like, but it is the done thing at the convent and so I go to see her.

'I've got a pash on you, can I make your bed?'

I know she thanks me and I remember making her bed once or twice, with help, but being the flipperty-gibbert I am, I soon lose interest. Some girls though seem to have a genuine passion for the older students. (I believe it was all quite harmless.)

I have few friends at the convent apart from Jeannie Robertson with her gammy leg, who always smells of urine, and who lives in Que Que with her elderly parents. I speak about her earlier in this memoir. I use poor Jeannie, a polio victim, while at the convent because she gets wonderful tuck from her parents. When her parcels arrive filled with chocolates, biscuits and items we never see, I am always by Jeannie's side only too willing to eat her comestibles. Other than that I barely speak to her, seeking friendship and approval elsewhere. I remember Jeannie's mother speaking to Pat about her disappointment in my duplicitous behaviour towards Jeannie. When Mum asks me about it I strenuously deny everything.

'I never did, honest Mum, I never ate all her stuff and went to another friend'.

Occasionally we see a film. On Friday or Saturday night we troop into the assembly hall to see either *Lassie* or *Lassie Come Home*. I love the dog, with his soft eyes and playful nature, but the story is sad. I find it so upsetting, I howl throughout the picture and when I go to bed I cry myself to sleep. I don't think I ever had a happy day or night at that place.

•

Mum and Dad visit occasionally. Mum always dresses to the nines. The girls make comments about her.

'Gee, your Mum's smart'.

One time, in particular, she arrives dressed in an apple green suit, jewels showing off her smooth throat and a wide brimmed cream hat and matching green hat band. She looks stunning. The girls stare and mutter among themselves. I am so embarrassed, I wish I could just disappear. Why didn't Mum look more ordinary, like the other mothers? This is the abiding memory of Mum's visits and her outfits and the reaction they cause. Somehow her elegance makes me more of an outsider. But all the same I wish she came to see more often. Oh! how I long to see her. I miss her more than Dad.

Eventually, all things pass and at the end of the school year our class teacher says to me,

'Romola, you have done very well, you have come second, but of course you *will* go to all these extra activities, I think you should give them up. Next year', she looks down at my report, 'No more extra curriculars'.

Shivers, at least my interests enable me to get away from the convent.

During that year I have once more taken up my great love – ballet, and go into town for my practices to a large hall with dozens of other children. We wear black ballet all-in-ones and study ourselves in the long floor-length mirrors. Most of us are little girls though there are a few boys. We do our *pleàs* knees bending to the floor, toes turned out, arms down to the side, up in front and then into a nice circle above our heads, and then repeat the whole movement as gracefully as we can. First position, second position, third position and fourth. Every child learning ballet remembers this by rote. We follow the Cecchetti school of instruction. I love ballet and am going to be a star like Margot Fonteyn. I think I am very good at arabesques.

One day our instructor says, 'Romola's ready for her points'.

I am so excited. I don't remember asking Mum and Dad for the shoes but they duly arrive.

'You must bathe your feet in methylated spirits to toughen the skin'.

I dream of fame and fortune. I can see myself dressed in white, swirly, floaty material, music soaring to the heavens and my feet arched in beautiful points. The reality is very different, I had not counted on pain and clumsiness and in the end it is all to no avail, because the instructor at the ballet school puts me on points too early which causes a deformation of my toes. During one of my Mum's visits she takes me to the doctor in Bulawayo, he studies my toes. I don't know what he tells Mum, but on the way back to the convent she says, 'Borgs, you must give up dancing, your toes will be ruined if you continue'.

Misery assails me and I never dance again.

So many horrible things happen at the convent, I could not relate them all. The year lasted a thousand years and when it ends, I beg my parents to take me from there. I remember nagging and crying throughout the Christmas holidays whenever the subject arises. Mum is resolved I should stay, but Ted, (bless him) decides I should leave and go back to the local school. He gets his way, and so it came to pass. An end to a truly awful time in my young life which, had it gone on, would have resulted in a complete breakdown.

•

The next year I return to the Que Que Public School and stay for a year and a bit. I am shy in the beginning and feel I have missed a lot and that all the children have established a circle of friends already, but gradually, I start seeing the girls whom I'd known before I went to the Convent. It is at this stage that I become friendly with Lindy Jones, and her sister Pat. During the time I had been away a new senior boarding school had been built over the road from the Residency. Also, there is a new place for swimming, one with an

Olympic-size pool and lovely manicured grassy surrounds. It is very smart, we think, and our little gang goes there constantly. We swim, lie on the hot concrete surrounds, eat copious quantities of ice-cream and engage with the boys (naturally!)

One school holiday I work at the OK Bazaars which has opened in the town on the main road to Salisbury, where once a café and block of flats had been. It is the days of synthetic fabrics, particularly nylon – Courtaulds is the manufacturer. The women in the shop who serve the customers speak about the advent of this wonder, 'nylon'.

'Nylon', one of them announces, 'Is so transparent, if a woman wears a nylon blouse and has her photo taken, you'll see her naked flesh'.

Of course this is all rubbish, but we believe every word of it, and talk endlessly about it. We speculate about our mothers appearing naked in nylon and as our parents have parties and take photos, I beg Mum not to buy this fabric. She asks why? I tell her and she laughs heartily. 'What nonsense', she says. I only half believe her.

The OK Bazaars (unlike today where shops display discreet price ticketing attached to a band on the edge of the counter); has the prices of their goods on tickets, attached to ticket stands, which are about eight-feet high. If you look across the OK Bazaars, you see no merchandise, just a veritable plethora of white tickets writ large! I am in the underwear section and several of my friends are there too. Mum is absolutely horrified. She says that no daughter of hers should be seen working in a place like the OK Bazaars! At the end of the school holidays she forbids me to go back. I am certain the OK management is more than pleased to get rid of me, because we talk, giggle and muck about a great deal among ourselves which annoys management. In other words we are a pretty hopeless bunch of kids.

•

During this time Mum and Dad separate. Mum loses complete interest in her home and everything around her. Her beloved garden is full of dead blooms. A deep depression overtakes her. She tells me later she suffers from strange delusions. At night under darkness her fingers become as huge as bananas and she often feels as though her bed is a little tiny object in the corner of a huge, frightening room. She also has pains in her head as though a steel band encircles her skull. All the symptoms of anxiety and stress. However, I do not know she is planning to leave us, but one day she takes me to the bank where she draws £250, with which she buys a little black Morris Minor, gets a job and moves to the Sebakwe Hotel. I call in to see her at her place of work where she is sitting in a minute room overlooking the street, behind a black typewriter. I have nothing to say to her nor she to me. Not understanding young people, she never forgives me because I sing Kay Starr's 'The Wheel of Fortune', over and over during the visit and feign disinterest. I remember that very well. What did I feel? I do not know, I only knew that Mum was leaving us to our fate.

Mum moves from the Sebakwe Hotel and lives for a while in a quaint cottage west of Que Que, across the golf course, not far from the Van Rynevelds. It is built on two levels. The bedrooms are at the top and then there are steps down into the garden and straight into the kitchen, dining room and living room. I occasionally go to stay there but am deeply unhappy.

'Mum why have you left us? Dad says everyone is talking about our family and they all blame you'.

She gets very angry.

'You don't know what you are talking about, Borgie'. Eyes aflashing: 'I can't put up with Edward anymore, and let me tell you, young lady, anyone who knows what Edward is like takes my part entirely'.

I'd start crying and though I am supposed to stay the weekend, I invariably got home to the Residency on Sundays. It is a sad time indeed. I hate this episode in my life. I am sure Mum does too. Both John and I feel Dad has been treated badly and he makes sure we continue feeling like that. Dad is and was a great manipulator.

Sometime later Mum meets my future step-father, Tony (Anthony Vernon Bradshaw), at a cocktail party at the Golf Club. Dad is furious about Mum and Tony. He makes many nasty, caustic remarks, and we stay on with him at the Residency.

I briefly want to mention the day my parents get divorced. The case, a custody battle and therefore contested, was heard in the Supreme Court in Bulawayo. The only thing the Judge was interested in was the welfare of us children. He took us aside and asked us where we wanted to live. Both of us say we'd prefer to live with our Dad. A woman who leaves her children was poorly regarded, and so Dad gets custody of us. Both Mum and Tony are flabbergasted. Dad was very jealous of Tony, furious with Mum and getting us vindicated him, or so he thought. But of course there were unforeseen consequences.

Anthony Vernon Bradshaw (Tony), while at London School of Mines

For all his failings, Dad is more understanding of children than my mother. And at that stage, Dad shows few signs of his dependence on alcohol and amphetamines. But I am lonely without Mum, deeply sad in fact. I miss seeing her walking around the garden, her big floppy hat concealing her face as she clips flowers for decorating of the lounge. I can see her sitting in the lounge reading, instructing the servants, all those little things. The house seems so big and empty. I grow despondent.

•

Dad is worried about me and contacts the Department of Education. I am still attending Que Que High School, but it is suggested that I go to Guinea Fowl, a school on the outskirts of Gwelo, where unhappy and disturbed children are sent. Of course, there were many children from stable backgrounds, some of whom came from the territories and regions of Southern and Northern Rhodesia and Nyasaland, as they were called then, but there are just as many like me.

— 10 —

Guinea Fowl

It's Valentine's Day, and like every Valentine Riva and I receive many cards between us, as do the other girls in Stirling House. We have many expectations of the day and slit open the pristine envelopes addressed to us. Out fall these great big red padded hearts with coy verses. They really are vulgar and gross, but we love receiving them. We laugh exultantly.

'Wonder who sent this one?'

'Hey, look at this, "Be My Valentine – from a secret admirer"'.

'Could it be Bill? I think he likes you'.

'No not Bill, perhaps Jack F'.

'Let's stick 'em on the window sill'.

I have no idea who sent me Valentine cards, neither does Riva and we take these all for granted. We like the boys and the boys liked us. QED, Valentine cards arrive!

•

We were both 'hitched', meaning we were *going steady* most of our school days. The first real boyfriend I had was Joe Viljoen, a stocky, sandy-haired, rugby player. He was in the same year as I but had an older brother called Clem. Most days we met in the rondavel outside the canteen at about 3pm. This structure had a short wall all around with wooden pole uprights supporting the thatched roof. We'd sit there talking for hours, or walk around the school grounds. The school's attitude to walking with your boyfriend was that you should 'keep walking'. A good maxim! At any time during the weekends you could see couples doing the Guinea Fowl stroll! Ronnie Rainsford who was already 18 years-old supplanted Joe. I was immensely proud of the fact that I had a boyfriend 3 years older than I. Ronnie was one of eleven Rainsford children whose family lived in Selukwe, a rather eccentric hamlet close to the school[27]. There were always a couple of Rainsfords, both girls and boys at Guinea Fowl at any one time. However, Ronnie, being a

---

[27] According to the *Lonely Planet* (1999) it is now called Shurugwi and is one of the better midlands towns today. Selukwe has one of the world's richest deposits of chromium ore.

senior, left the school at the end of my first year. I was then 'hitched' to Gary Latilla. Mum described this as 'concentrating' and was opposed to this 'concentrating' on any particular person. As his name suggests he was of Italian extraction, with black, curly hair, brown eyes and a small scar on his rather pouty lips. I thought he was gorgeous. His mother had been married several times and he was brought up by his grandparents, who lived in Marandellas. During one Christmas school holiday his grandfather died. Gary was deeply upset by this, his feelings of security badly shaken. This relationship with Gary went on until I left school and for about a year after that, so it lasted about four years in all. I have a photo of him circa 1956 in the 1st Rugby XV from the 1956 School Magazine.[28]

Teenagers do crazy things, especially as far as boys are concerned. As it is now so it was then. One term at school there was a craze for sucking dummies! Truly. There we were, 15 year olds, running around with great big dummies in our mouths. Trouble was we laughed so much while drawing attention to ourselves, cackling away, all teeth and streaming eyes, the dummies fell out. Our teachers showed admirable restraint, not one of them made a comment and this, in an age, where children should be seen and not heard. The philosophy of the school was ahead of its time; instead of punishing us for our stupidity we were just ignored. Anyway this phase didn't last long, for soon we were blonding our hair. Today's young women get all their make-up and hair colouring tips from a plethora of magazines. For us it is difficult to find anything of that nature, no women's magazines cross our desks. We found out about bleaching hair quite by accident, and naturally, we did this to impress the boys. We'd spend hours 'doing our roots' and then pouring and combing the bleach through our hair. It stung the tender skin on our necks and the dripping bleach was painful. After a few months we have grassy textured hair, quite awful to feel and impossible to comb. So bleaching met the fate of all the other fads and we gave it up. (Once again there was no intervention from the staff).

•

If the convent was hell, Guinea Fowl is the complete opposite. For gone is fear and religiosity, suppression and bigotry. What you may well ask turns my life around in such a spectacular manner? My being at Guinea Fowl starts because

---

[28] After attempting to find Gary for a long time which entailed looking through the White Pages for both Zimbabwe and South Africa I found a listing which was his daughter's fax number. She told me by email he had died in an industrial accident in 1984.

as mentioned earlier, Dad's friend in the Education Department recommends this school. We, that is Dad, John and I arrive at Guinea Fowl on a sunny Saturday afternoon. We drive along the stripped Selukwe road southeast from Gwelo, and parallel to the railway line which is on our left-hand side. About 17kms along the way I notice buildings on the right and ahead of us, some are demountables and others have tin roofs catching the afternoon sun and set among the trees. The whole area is an open grassy vista.

'That's the school', says Dad.

He turns left gently over the track, and turning right at the first round-about skirts the main area of the school, driving slowly along a tarred road. We pass what I later learn is the gymnasium, to a building with a gray tin roof and netted verandah set in a mature and jungly-style garden. This is the home of the Headmaster and his wife, the Ferrers. Mr Ferrer had been a Lieutenant-Colonel during the Second World War, and is the first headmaster of the school. His daughters, named Ann and Jill (although I don't know this at the time), are practising different pieces on, perhaps, a cello and a piano, so the house is filled with the cacophony of clashing chords.

'Hullo'. Dad and I shake hands with this tall, dark haired person, the very neatly attired Headmaster. He smiles at me.

'Sorry about the noise, the girls have to practice'. He is silent and looks intently at me, as if he were sizing me up. 'I think you will like it here'.

We sit on the veranda. Long Savannah type grass which extends to the horizon waves slightly in the warm sunlight. There is the gentle undertow, faintly discernible of insect sounds. It is quite soporific and I feel a little drowsy. Mrs Ferrer makes tea and brings us a plate of scones with jam. She looks at me.

'You'll be with Lillian'.

I nod dutifully. I have no idea who 'Lillian' might be. About half an hour later the girls, their practice finished, join us. They look a serious pair to me in their brown-rimmed spectacles and short brown hair. One of them is pretty. They smile at me and drink their tea. Shortly after this we drive to what is to be my home-from-home for the next five years.

In one of its previous existences, for there had been a few, and apart from the fact that there had been a gold mine called Guinea Fowl on the site, this school had been a Flying Squad training base in 1940. Its official name was No 2 F.I.S. Guinea Fowl. Corrugated iron and wood barrack-rooms, kitchen, messes, water supply, sanitation and recreation facilities for 700 men, necessitated a rail siding to be constructed for the arrival of heavy equipment. Later, plans were drawn up to convert Guinea Fowl into a school, originally taking male pupils only, and in 1947 the first intake of students arrived. The following year the school started enrolling girls. The entire surplus, albeit temporary, buildings were used as classrooms, dining halls, academic block and hostels. These were nothing like the grand, sandstone buildings usually associated with schools.

•

The first thing I notice is an enormous gray tin building with a domed roof which looms over all the others. A large green pepper tree grows beside it, half as tall as the roof line. I am told it was once part of the aircraft mechanical workshops, and is now used for the school's laundry which is managed by a Mrs Fischer. Her husband oversees the place, and is the first caretaker. The Fishers have been at the school since before its inception and Mr Fisher puts a good many years of his life into the place. All the hostels at this co-educational school are named after bombers from World War Two as a tribute to the Royal Air Force. The girls live in Stirling and York both of which are surrounded by a sturdy fence, topped with barbed wire. The Stirling girls don't mix much with students in York and vise-versa. I recall the name of only one girl from York who played in the 1st XI hockey and who made her dislike of me very apparent. The boys live in Lancaster, Blenheim, Lincoln and Wellington. Two of the boys' hostels are set in a block which is the nucleus of the main section of the school and which resembles a small town criss-crossed by sealed roads. The remaining boys' hostels (Lincoln and Blenheim) are located about a mile away from the main block at the site of the original Flying Training School's married quarters that also became the residential part of the School of Mines for a few years. This is referred to as 'bottom school'. Every day the boys who live there traipse across the rail line, through the grassy fields, up the hill to get to classes or to play sport or attend the canteen.

I am in Stirling. The brick building is a low, ranch-style surrounded by jacarandas which are planted outside the encircling wire fence in the front and inside at the back. Every November they come into bloom – a spectacular sight. On the northern end of the building are five dormitories which you enter via a glass door. These 'dorms' as we call them, run off the left-hand side of a long corridor which elevates slightly from one end to the other. They are built in a fretwork style, with a grassy area and washing lines at the back and between each of the five. Locker rooms extend to the right from the entrance of each individual dormitory. Juniors are housed in the first dormitory next to the glass doors. These young students sleep soundlessly (without a murmur) during their nocturnal slumbers. The older girls in the other dorms toss and turn, sigh, groan and cry out in their sleep, an interesting and unexplained phenomenon. At the end of the elevation are greeny glass tiles built into the wall which bring a little light into what is a very dark building. Opposite the first dormitory and across the corridor is the ablution block with a serried row of basins and windows overlooking a grassy section. Behind the basins are rows of cubicles with baths. To the right of them, the toilets. The girls visiting the toilets refer to this as 'going to "chong"', as in 'I want to go to "chong"'. At the rear is a small room, a sort of entrance, with pigeon holes filled with shoes. Outside is a large incinerator. When the incinerator is activated the boys walking in the street shout, 'Burning your sanitary towels, are ya?'

    We cringe because the acrid smell leaves no-one in doubt as to its purpose.

    The hostel prefects have four separate rooms away from the dorms and, therefore, from the rest of us, where they sleep and study. This enables them to revise for their examinations whenever they want, day or night. I envy them and look forward to the day, should it arrive, when I too can move into one of the individual rooms. At the southern end of the boarding section is the prep room where all of us sit week-nights to do our homework. The house mistress is a Mrs Nixon, (Lillian, so this is the 'Lillian'), an attractive blonde woman with rather colourless bulging eyes which sometimes look light green, thin lips, a small chin close to her mouth; she is middle-aged and pale-skinned. A soft-hearted woman who sometimes finds us hard going. She's widowed with two red-headed children. They live in a garden flat off the prep room which one accesses through a small office containing a small table and the telephone where we speak to our parents when they call us. There is an internal wire fence over which a granadilla[29] plant grows profusely. This fence separates her quarters from the rest of the House.

    Also residing on the premises is the matron, Miss Dorothy Burns, whom we seldom see; a short, dumpy woman with a Southern English twang to her

---

[29] Passionfruit.

voice. When she smiles, which is often, her eyes disappear into folds and she has a decidedly Oriental expression. She has a fondness for an emerald green cardigan, which Rhodesians call a 'jersey', and wears red carpet slippers. She has bunions. She smokes a good deal while organising the laundry, so that every week we get fresh sheets, pillows and towels with a faint odour of tobacco. You enter her apartment from the same central corridor, and once inside you walk down a passage past the laundry closet to her living quarters. The front of her flat, with its small pretty garden overlooks the main road which runs through the school up to the Science Laboratory, the administration block and the large assembly hall. I believe Ms Burns worked at Guinea Fowl until it closed in 1978.

Like all Rhodesian school children, we wear a school uniform. The dress in summer is blue, which I rather like. The winter uniform is a pleated pinafore in navy serge with hideous lisle stockings, which wrinkle like a concertina in an unbecoming fashion, and a navy blazer. Our distinctive badge is the Guinea Fowl on a navy blue background.

The boys wear khaki in both summer and winter but long dark gray trousers, with a white shirt, school tie and navy blazer for best dress.

Guinea Fowl School Badge

Students, Friends and Others I Knew

Wilma Landsman was my first friend at Guinea Fowl. I was very fond of Wilma, with her dark hair cut in a fringe and her rather prominent lips, she had a laugh full of cheeriness; she seemed to be all that was wise and beautiful. She came from a country town somewhere to the north of the country. We were in dorm 1 and she slept in one of the gray iron beds with the regulation gray blankets at the end of the room on the right hand side. I suppose she was about a year older than I. But Wilma left the school at the end of 1952. I often thought about her after she had gone, and many years later met up with her in Salisbury in 1969, she had married a policeman – strangely, we had nothing in common anymore.

Then Riva Smith, from Nyasaland (Malawi) became my new best friend. Riva was one of four girls in her family. Her oldest sister Peta was a couple of years ahead of us. The other sisters were named Erica and Lesley because their father was hoping for a boy at each birth, hence these rather masculine names. Riva, however, was named after an old flame of her father's. She was attached to her father and told me a lot about him. Riva was very attractive, not to say beautiful. Dark widely spaced expressive hazel eyes and a wide mouth and lovely teeth. She had wavy hair, rather similar to my own hair and was given to plumpness but was so confident and merry, no-one noticed, as she had oodles of what they call today, charisma. Also, she was a bright girl and excelled in whatever she did, both at school and in her adult life, though she was not in the least sporty.

A pair of show-offs: Riva and me, 1956

We are rebels, there's no doubting it. The students find the way Riva and I behave difficult to comprehend. But, we have a lot of fun. We have no need for other girl friends in the early days and are a roguish pair. Later we become friendly with Jane Williamson, who eventually marries a farmer and lives at Triangle Sugar Estate. Riva remembers being friendly with the Bousefield girls, Marion and Ann. They are rather vague personalities to me, but one has sandy hair and freckles.

We are overly interested in boys at age fifteen, at which time we have been at the school a couple of years and have many young male friends. There is Alan Stein, ('Yank' to us) with his American accent, a tall, lanky individual we like a lot. He is a lot more sophisticated than the rest of us, and has an exotic quality because of his nationality and accent. I hadn't met an American up to that time, apart from Victor Putz that is, who lived with his American parents in Que Que in the late 1940s and early 1950s, and who was very young. We did't know the expression 'cool' then, but that's what Al was, 'cool'. Yank's brother-in-law was in the United States Marines which makes Yank even more interesting to us. He tells us lots of stories about that defence force so far away from Rhodesia. He also makes a deep impression upon me by telling me a woman's body was what he notices first.

'What about their faces?' I ask, amazed!

'No, no, their bodies that's what matters, I never notice their faces', he insists.

He obviously knows something that none of us know and therefore becomes even more fascinating. When he leaves school he works at Duly's Garage in Bulawayo as an apprentice mechanic and sometime thereafter returns to the United States where he lives today. Next up is Hilton Sidney Burleigh Arthur Godbolt Cole with his curly hair and his thick 'Coca-Cola glasses' who lives in Selukwe. He always has a Nagapie[30] about his person. Many of the boys have these animals for pets at Guinea Fowl. Hilton loves to talk and with his glasses glinting in the sun he is definitely nerdy. Robert McIlwaine was someone we knew quite well. He never tells me, and I never ask, if he is related to the McIlwaine family after whom Lake McIlwaine in

---

[30] Galago Moholi - Lesser Bushbabies who prefer wooded areas. Bushbabies are adorable in appearance with their long, furry tail, large expressive eyes, cute ears and soft, light grey wooly fur, and are nocturnal animals.

Salisbury is named. He is Jane Williamson's boyfriend and always dances with her at canteen. He is six foot tall with dark hair and the bluest eyes. When he leaves school, Robert joins one of the government agencies in Salisbury. No-one knows what he does. When I bumped into him in Salisbury in 1969 he was secretive and guarded. He had an air of importance about him and was inscrutable. I felt I could not have a conversation with him, as he was so tight-lipped. An intelligence operative perhaps? Perhaps he was hiding things. This was disconcerting in the extreme.

Another personality from our school days, Theunis de Klerk an Afrikaans boy with very dark eyes and skin is the Head Prefect in 1955. He is marked for great things, for he has 'leadership qualities', everybody says so. (Apparently, after he left school he went to work at Salisbury airport and did something quite ordinary for a while, but eventually became a Member of Parliament. Sadly, he died during the Rhodesian war of African independence in the mid-1970s.)

Peter Wilson and I are both prefects in 1956. He is a short person, a little effeminate, with an open face and dun coloured close cropped curly hair. He has a sister at school called Pam, a blond, but we do not know her well although she is also in Stirling. She is a little younger than Riva and I.

An unusual personality is Garth Hewitt. He is lanky, has equally lanky black hair, black eyes and a pixie face. He is ungainly on the sports field. Dressed in his shorts, he looks for all the world like a flightless crow as he makes ineffectual stabs at tennis which sets us into fits of giggles. His first few years at school are unremarkable but at about age 15 he blossoms and starts coming first in class! From then on we take Garth Hewitt seriously and stop laughing at him because of his peculiar looks.

Another person in our circle of friends is Kevin Thompson. He has dark burnished red hair and a Scottish complexion, the type that doesn't like the sun. When Kevin smiles his mouth became a wide oval, flattened top and bottom. He is a rugby player. When we meet he nicknames me 'dolls' cheeks'. He gazes at me and laughs, 'Where *did* you get those rosy dolls' cheeks?' Kevin often meets Riva and me for a chat and dances with us in canteen. When he left school he went to Sandhurst, and was one of the very few people at Guinea Fowl that I see later on, as I met him in London.

(I heard quite recently he died in a balloon accident having quit the army and gone to America.)

Buller Carstens did history with us. He is a so shy, he can't look anyone in the face. We never get to know him well but tease him because his moniker is the same as General Buller, someone we learnt about in history. Poor boy, be blushes furiously. However, despite the fact he is so inarticulate and self-effacing, he plays good rugby, making the Guinea Fowl first XV in 1956.

Another boy who looms large in my life is Twig Wood, a boy whose parents live close to the school. His mother, Daphne, is 'hearty', and so is Twig. He has a gold filling in one of his front teeth. (I last heard of Twig in 1969. He was living in Harare and working for Rothmans' Tobacco).

Peter T was a person whose treatment at the collective hand of all of us is something I regret. I would like to apologise to him. I do not remember particularly why we despise him. He is not appealing in the slightest, but we shouldn't have 'hissed' at him at every opportunity. He is teased so much it amounts to verbal abuse. (I wonder why the teachers were unaware of his undoubted unhappiness at the hands of his school mates? If they were, they made no attempt to help the poor boy.)

Finally, I vividly recall Bill Lindfield, a handsome lad, who knew he was good-looking. After school he joined the Rhodesian police, and I wonder where he is today.

•

I have a photo of the 1956 1st X1 Hockey team. There we are, our hair cropped to below the ears, short hair was fashionable then. Jackie Jarvis, Esmé Purvis, Anna Coetzer, all sporty in some way or another. Jackie is a great swimmer, Esmé, you can see in the photo, is tall and blond and Anna, an Afrikaans girl, (she always pipped me in athletics). My old friend from my days in Que Que, Julie Theron is there too. We had grown apart in High School and I no longer hung around with her. In the back row is Janet Patterson, she always looks terrific in her hockey outfit because she has such good legs.

Apart from those of us who are good at sports, there is a pair of sisters called Hutchinson. Fay, the elder, has hair blond as wheat and her younger sister's hair was like wire-iron. I have never seen a pair to dissimilar. Their mother was murdered, a great shock as you can imagine to both of them and to us.

Valerie Irlam, I wonder where Valerie is? One evening after prep, someone comes to fetch her while she is preparing for bed, I see her crying in the dormitory and packing her bags and then, without a goodbye she is gone, just like that. Rumour has it that her parents split up. I saw Valerie years later on Muizenberg beach, Cape Town, still as pretty as she was at school.

These then were some of the many people who filled the landscape of my life at Guinea Fowl during the 1950s. There were many others whose names I recall, but whose faces have faded with time, people like Elizabeth Zietsman, Josephine Hill, Deleen Humphreys, Kay Salter; all that is left are scraps – dark hair, a half-forgotten incident, blue eyes. I wish I could conjure them from my faulty filing system.

Guinea Fowl was a sports mad school. Rugby Union, hockey, tennis, athletics, swimming, squash and cross-country running. Many boys did the cross-country, a five mile run for seniors and three for juniors which during the first term of the year was undertaken about four times per week. The boys played rugby against sides from schools such as Plumtree, Tech and Milton in Bulawayo and Prince Edward and Allan Wilson[31] in Salisbury. Once a year, the Chaplin/Guinea Fowl rugby clash took place. Chaplin was our rival! We never missed a match.

Occasionally the 1st XV played against a South African school, which was a big event. A bit like the Americans coming for rest and recreation in Sydney during the war. I imagine everyone was twittering with excitement to see these good-looking young men walking about. Sometime later, I read that Mrs Nixon said, about a visit by a Natal Rugby side: 'Great joy among the girls, for it was a case of "off with the old love and on with the new"'.[32]

Of course we were not supposed to fraternize at all with the South African lads. But there was an almost palpable frisson at matches where they were playing.

The Guinea Fowl Sports weekend was the highlight of the sporting calendar. This was held on the playing fields outside the sports pavilion. Parents, friends, siblings, all arrived by car or train for the event. The whole school too watched us. There was a gala atmosphere. The school looked its very best, newly washed and pristine. Invariably it was hot and dusty. I recall perspiring a great deal on every sports day without exception, but for all that I loved sports day as I was athletic; the runner up for the *victrix laudorum* two years in a row. Trouble was, I was a dud at long-jump and Anna Coetzee (the star of athletics, a little, skinny, blond Afrikaans girl I have mentioned already)

---

[31] Allan Wilson (1856 – 4 December 1893), was born in Scotland. He is best known for his leadership of the Shangani Patrol which resulted in his death and made him a national hero in Rhodesia.(Wikipedia)
[32] Anecdote taken from www.guineafowlschool.com/history. Information taken from *Schools of Rhodesia*.

beat me every time to the top prize. After I left Guinea Fowl and while living in Johannesburg I returned one sports weekend in 1957. That was the only time I visited the school again.

We looked forward to the school gymkhanas as well. I won the diving competition. Jackie Jarvis who was an excellent swimmer and diver herself gave me some valuable tips which helped me enormously. Riva and I became quite friendly with Jackie and her brother Chris to whom Riva was 'hitched' for a short time. From the day I left school I never dived again, neither did I play hockey or participate in athletics. I think it is because my life opened up in so many different ways, especially once I got to the United Kingdom, that my interest in sports, like so many other interests in my childhood, just vanished.

I love gymnastics. The horse, parallel bars and ropes are a challenge, the *twhwack* and *thump* of students and instructors landing as they came down from the equipment and the exaggerated sound with its echoey quality, all due to the vaulted shape of the room, in which we practice. I challenge and test myself and became stronger and more flexible with every term.

FIRST ELEVEN HOCKEY

In 1956, while in the 1st XI hockey team where I play left wing, I receive my hockey colours. I am proud of my pale blue blazer with trim in red and blue and the Guinea Fowl badge on the pocket.

One year we catch the train at Gwelo station and are away for the whole weekend visiting the Umtali High School for the inter-school hockey trials. Umtali is in the mountainous region of Zimbabwe, and is a beautiful area of the country. Those very high mountains provided hiding places for the wartime guerillas during the 1960s and 1970s and during that time the area was no longer safe, especially for whites. However, there is no inkling of things to come that hockey weekend. The dormitory where the team sleeps seems to be right under a mountain, or maybe in the shadow, so crisp and cool was the air. Imagine my disappointment when, after the trials, I am not chosen for the national team, being hopelessly outclassed by my opposite left wing's play. I realise that my abilities on the hockey field are rather ordinary compared to others. It was just not good enough to merely be a big fish in a small pond.

FIRST FIFTEEN RUGBY

We also sing at Guinea Fowl. The assembly hall which is close to the headmaster's office and other administration buildings is the place chosen for this.

'I want you all to learn Nymphs and Shepherds', says our singing teacher to the class.

'Nymphs and Shepherds!' The boys are horrified. Anything as sissy as such a title puts them off immediately. She also wants us to learn a most inappropriate song which came straight from the rugby fields of English Public Schools, probably Eton.

I remember a line or two of this song:

Follow up, follow up, follow up, 'til the fields ring again and again.
With the tramp of the twenty-two men – follow up, follow up.

At least it has a good rhythm. Then there is a song we regard as definitely poncy, all about Phoebus, or Phoebe, or Cressida or Croesus. I don't remember the tune, but it is dreary and we do not like it. One term it's mooted that we sing Handel's *Messiah*. I remember all the practicing we did, especially for 'The Halleluah Chorus' and 'For Unto Us a Son is Born'. This goes on for a few months, and then, for an unknown reason, at least none is given to us, it is announced that the whole project be scrapped. Nobody queries it, we just accept that we will not be performing the *Messiah*. Accepted the way most young people accept anything they are told. Singing seems to stop in the later years.

If I am good at sports, my school work is not up to scratch. I am hopeless at maths and science but comfortable with history, art and English. One of our English teachers that actually stays on a length of time has a Scottish name and moles on her face, and is a stickler for parsing. We spend hours taking sentences apart, which unlike most students I enjoy. Clauses, sub-clauses, adjectival nouns, tenses, all are fascinating. She instills in me a love of the language. Sentence analysis in its own way is a precise geometry. I also study Latin: *amo, amas, amat, amamus, amatus, amant* etc. etc. I loathe it, but today I am sorry I did not persevere, dropping out after one year. Mr Muir took the maths' dunces, like me, for book-keeping and arithmetic. He has floppy thin sandy hair, wears glasses, brown suits and thick-soled brown shoes. Our lessons are in an oval-shaped corrugated iron room opposite Stirling House (the original Chapel). Mr Court, our geography teacher, with his black slightly wavy hair, black moustache and thin build, always wears pale suits, either light brown or fawn which, I suppose, were rather becoming. He drills into us the Beaufort Wind Scale – which I still remember – and was keen to teach us topography. Ox-bow formations in rivers and the like. Not much else has been retained from his teaching, though I have no doubt it was not his fault.

At this school you can either learn Afrikaans or French. Riva elects to do French, and I, Afrikaans. Our Afrikaans teacher is Meneer Wagenaar, curly-haired, he is a beefy individual with a penchant for jackets with leather elbow inserts. I loathe Afrikaans and Meneer totally ignores me. 'Snave', (Mr Talbot Evans) the history master and house master of Wellington, develops the debating society and teaches us British history. Although we do a little American-British history (I remember the Boston Tea Party), his speciality, is the British Raj; Clive of India, suttee,[33] the black hole of Calcutta; the Sepoys objecting to removing bullets by mouth because they had been rubbed around with pig fat and other events Indian. Come to think of it, he probably was in the army himself.[34] He has a military bearing with pale brushed-back hair and an equally pale moustache. He is an elegant-looking man with a clipped English voice. However, there is not a thing taught about the history of Africa or the Africans. We know that Mzilikazi and Lobengula had been kings but that was all. Everything I subsequently learned about the blacks of Rhodesia and South Africa and other parts of the Continent was 20 years down the track. My Australian friends tell me the real history of Australia and Aboriginal dispossession was not taught to them either and only brought to their attention in the late 1980s with the 'Bringing them Home' investigation and book about the phenomenon.

Art, now that's a subject I thoroughly enjoy, especially under the tutelage of Mr Geoff Day. Sometime in 1953 he redesigned the Guinea Fowl badge incorporating the motto *Suaviter in Modo, Fortiter in Re*[35] together with six fleurs-de-lis for the six hostels, the shield being surmounted by the Guinea Fowl. His enthusiasm and interest in the artistic and cultural life of the school imbues many of us with a love of the arts. I believe he left in 1957.

Sometimes during term time we put on plays or concerts performed in the gymnasium, which is converted into a hall with banks of chairs for the performances. I never audition for the plays. Riva auditions and is successful in a number of roles. Some of the staff also get parts, depending on the play. The performances are great fun. One year the players put on *The Ghost Train*, good school fare. By all accounts it goes down well. I always offer to work back-stage and do the curtains. Of course I use the occasion to meet Gary and there are many opportunities behind stage in the billowing black

---

[33] The act of a Hindu widow willingly cremating herself on the funeral pyre of her dead husband.

[34] He had been in the Royal Marines, captured in Crete and a prisoner of war in WW2.

[35] Gentle in Manner, Vigorous in Deed.

curtains or outside the building for 'snogging'. At one of our school concerts in 1955, Riva, Jane Williamson, Gertie with her concertina and one other girl and I under the moniker The Stirling Starlets do a musical turn. Gertie accompanies us and we sing and dance to 'The Tennessee Wig-Walk': 'Put your toes together and your knees apart...' And 'Side-By-Side':

> Oh we ain't got a barrel of money,
> Maybe we're ragged and funny,
> But we'll travel along,
> Singing a song,
> Side-by-side.

The 'canteen', as this is euphemistically called, was the place where school dances are held. In its air force days it was a mess with a large central room with hatch (probably a bar), and small rooms on either side. Dancing is a favourite pastime and after Riva came to the school, we partner each other in our dancing lessons. We truly love practices and twirl and swirl, quite oblivious to our surroundings. I imagine dancing ever onwards, up into the clouds, landing on a Persian Flying Carpet. I remember the music we play: 'Unchained Melody'; 'Do Not Forsake Me, Oh, My Darling' (the theme from Gary Cooper's great western, *High Noon*), and other songs of that era are favourites.

On special 'canteen nights', out came our pale pink and blue water-marked taffeta dresses and frilled half-slips. Some of the girls favour lace bodices. A really smashing outfit is a pink lace top with full, flouncy taffeta skirt. For less formal occasions waffle pique or *broderie anglais* is the rage. The boys wear best dress (dark gray trousers and navy blazers) but leave their sports coats for informal occasions. We dance with the boys. Ballroom dancing it is, and both sexes are good at that, for tripping the light fandango has a certain social caché, and boosts your social life. Canteen nights are full of fun and jollity. We like senior canteen because the older boys dance with us. We are never wallflowers!

Later, when I am a senior and organise the dances with a couple of senior boys it became a time of responsibility and isn't as much fun.

Every meal time we line up in twos and walk across to the dining room supervised by one of the staff, while the boys from Lancaster and Wellington, also in crocodile, wait for us to go past. There is something enjoyable about that simple exercise, walking past the boys. There are two dining halls for the four houses at the top school. The food is pretty execrable, egg slosh for breakfast which is disgusting and made from powdered egg, and slimy stews for dinner. However, we occasionally get real butter from the teacher who sits at the head of the table. She chooses one of us to pass this uneaten morsel, quite democratically as it turns out. Over a week we each get a turn. You have no idea how we look forward to that pat of butter for it is not long after WW2 rationing. To this day I think there is nothing quite like the comfort food of butter. Thoughts of comfort food naturally make me think of the school tuck-shop which is located opposite the boys' hostels on the way to the dining room. However, I have a better and more varied supply of goodies because I bought chocolates and sweets on Dad's account – that is while he is living in Fort Victoria, so probably 1955. Once he started receiving his monthly statements showing my extravagant purchases of yummy food, he put a stop to my 'on tick' purchases.

The first time I see a person suffering anorexia is at Guinea Fowl, but we have no idea why this particular girl is so thin as the condition is virtually unknown. She is in York House and had been pleasantly plump. I see her in the mornings before breakfast waiting in line outside the dining hall. Every week she gets thinner and thinner. She wastes away before our eyes. I often wonder what happened to her. Quite coincidentally around that time I go into Gwelo for a haircut and there is a young blond hairdresser with the same stick-thin body, her bones protruding from her shoulders, a sight which reminds me of the pictures of the Belsen inmates. Little do we know anorexia will become a scourge in the western world among teenage girls.

The sick-bay for those who suffer malaria and flu is set away from the rest of the school at the southern end, and has lovely flame trees surrounding it. The beds are high off the floor and it is light and warm with large windows around the building. For convalescing there is no better place. You could lie in a therapeutic sun-filled ward watching the trees waving in the breeze, their trunks turning dark at sunset. Sister Knox, for there is only one, is a heavily built bosomy woman with a red face as if she has been at the port. She has no truck with school kids. She dishes out copious quantities of quinine for malaria or flu. I once spend time there, my ears ringing from the liberal doses of quinine, which naturally Sister Knox insists I take.

As you can see, the day-to-day school life is like every other school. To get to our various classrooms we traipse from one tin-roofed demountable to another as the school buildings are widespread. The day is broken up into periods in which are set the subjects we are studying. We always start with assembly in the main hall, where we say a daily prayer and where the Headmaster makes whatever announcements are on the agenda. We then go to different classrooms, depending on what we are studying at the time. In this way there is nothing different about the school. But in all other ways it is entirely unusual.

•

On Tuesdays the boys had cadets. They would suddenly appear in the afternoon, at about 3pm, from all over the school grounds, dressed in their military gear, some carrying drums and wind instruments; trumpets and bugles. We could hear them tooting away or occasionally banging a drum while they assembled on the grounds outside the very last classroom at the southern end of the school. The drill master barked out his commands:

   'Attention!'
   'Stanat ease!'
   'Quick march!'

Guinea Fowl cadets, 1956

The school brass band strikes up, they play 'It's a Long way to Tipperary', 'Scotland the Brave', 'Colonel Bogie' and other military classics from the

United Kingdom. It was a good military band. But, as you would expect, there was always someone out of tune providing a distracting discord. They marched back and forth, turning, standing to attention, the whole gamut of school-boy army ritual. After their exercises, at sunset, a lone trumpeter always played the Last Post. Then they dispersed, still playing military tunes. I loved brass-bands then and do today.

In true gender separation of the 1950s, Robert and Gary asked Riva and me if we would iron their cadet outfits. This was the done thing. We'd proudly take the brown shirts and shorts slaving away, trying to iron them properly. But as none of us had a clue about ironing we were pretty hopeless and took an inordinate time over it.

One year I suggested to Gary that I make a flag for the cadets.

'Good idea', he said, 'But where will you get the material?'

'Gwelo, when next I go there'.

So a large blue piece of material was purchased. I carefully cut it into a square, onto which I embroidered the school emblem. It took me a few weeks, but I look on that time with satisfaction because my efforts turned out quite well, especially when the flag was attached to a wooden pole and borne aloft for ceremonial occasions.

I cannot speak for all the students, but I was happy at Guinea Fowl as was Riva. It was a special place. Here was a co-ed school, all boarders, slap bang in the middle of the Rhodesian bush. It is difficult to express what going to this school meant in terms of freedom and soothing the soul. There were many children who came from other parts of Africa, like Malawi, Zambia or country Southern Rhodesia. Those country kids could not easily attend day school so boarding school was the answer for them. It was egalitarian and unpretentious. You walked in the playing fields to the south-east of the school and when the grass was cut and piled into large haystacks, you could lie in the hay with your own thoughts or sit in the sports pavilion, amble into the bush on the south side, or wander over the cricket pitch. A few farmers lived in the vicinity. The closest town to the south was the hamlet of Selukwe and to the north, Gwelo, home of our rival school, Chaplain. Guinea Fowl was a school of a type unknown today and probably there will never be another like it.

Guinea Fowl closed in 1978, at which time it was purely a boy's school, the girls having been phased out in 1958. For years afterwards I dreamt about the school. In my dreams I was still there, the oldest person around! During the transition the girls from York moved in to Stirling House but we did not know that would be the school's fate then. However, what enthralled us did not sit well with teachers and there was a high staff turnover. Probably the lack of academic rigor, isolation and parochialism got them down.

The maths, geography and history masters stayed a length of time as did our Physical Education teacher, Margot Boileau, who later played hockey for Rhodesia, and the Afrikaans teacher Wagenaar and the aesthetic, slim French teacher. As for the rest, they came and went. One character who was there for years, however, and who I remember well, was The Reverent Ivor Clark from Shabani. He was the religious instructor, and also taught English. We called him 'Ivor Boop'[36] because of his large stomach. But his claim to fame was not his instruction, but his appearance, and the fact that at every social event he sang a favourite song. He was bald, wore spectacles and sported a long, flowing white outfit, a sort of Kaftan, before they became fashionable. Every Sunday night after school prayers which were held in the assembly hall he would intone: 'May the Lord be with you and keep you and may the Lord make his face to shine upon you and give your peace. Ahhhhhmen!'

As for the ditty? It went like this:

My name is Solomon Levy and I live in Salem Street
That's where to buy your coats and vests and everything else that's neat.
Second handed ulsterettes and overcoats so fine, for all the boys who dine with me at one-forty-nine.
Oh Solly Levy, lala la alala.
Poor Solly Levy, lalalalallla (and so on)

We thought him a peculiar character, and although his song was amusing our interest in music was entirely different. Glen Miller's 'String of Pearls' was more our line. We immersed ourselves in American popular 'kulcha' (as Dad would derisively call it), went to the bioscope to see June Allyson and Debbie Reynolds with her pert features. Gary Latilla and I went to see *Tammy and the Bachelor* several times. It made a big impression. Every generation has its music. We were no exception. On Sunday nights after lights out we listened to *Hits of the Week from Mocambique*, with David Davies broadcasting from a radio station in Lourenco Marques, Portuguese East Africa. 'Cry' with Johnny Ray, Doris Day with her sweet, sugary voice, and 'The Lion Sleeps Tonight':

---

[36] Afrikaans slang for a large belly.

Way up boys, Wimmaway! Oh? Wimmaway wimmaway Oh! Wimmaway.
In the jungle, the mighty jungle, the lion sleeps tonight, etc.

This accompanied by a lot of wailing. There was also:

Ay-round the corner,
Ay-round the corner, hoo! hoo!,
Beneath the berry tree,
Around the foot paaath,
Behind the bush,
Looking for Henry Lee!

I hear these songs and am transported to Guinea Fowl circa 1954.

Coronation of Queen Elizabeth II

The year is 1953 and in a far-away country called Korea, on 27 July, the Armistice is signed; thereby ending four years of bloody warfare between north and south Korea. As we all know the division between the two Koreas lives on. In Britain, in the same year, in June, a new Queen is crowned, Elizabeth II, is as much admired in her day for her beauty as was Diana Princess of Wales in hers. I don't remember any formal celebration at the school although I am sure there was one, but on the day of Elizabeth's coronation we are given a holiday and naturally the whole school goes to Gwelo to Luna Park.

There we are. Luna Park celebrations appeal to us. It's set up in Gwelo. All school excursions are by bus to Gwelo. We wear our Sunday best and pile onto the bus which bowls down the stripped roads, which slowly melt in the hot sun under blue skies. We look out for One-Tree Hill, (aptly named because there is a single tree growing in the middle of the hill) and is about half-way between Guinea Fowl and Gwelo. All the while we sing 'Funagalo, Funagalo'. This African satirical song is based on the pigeon language that whites try to teach blacks working on the South African gold mines because, with their different languages, it is difficult for those from one tribe to communicate with people from different tribes with different languages. After much winding and turning, out of nowhere Gwelo is before us. At Luna Park we alight – a glittering day lies before us. All Riva's and my friends are there as well as our favourite teachers. The Big Wheel, the lights, the throngs of Rhodesians ambling about, coconut shies, the grinning clown heads, the whole gamut of the fair. Music blares, kids run about with Candy Floss on sticks or toffee-apples. Ice-cream sellers have a field day, no pun intended. We have turns on the coconut shire, and I believe win some rather gross toys and other merchandise.

We do not have the benefit of television to watch the proceedings. All communication comes from newspapers, the British and American newsreels which we see at the cinema and of course information is by telegram and telephone. We wait, possibly a week or two, to see the moment captured on *Gaumont British News* and *Movietone News* with their announcers speaking in very, very clipped tones, this being the preferred method of delivery. But see her we do. I am struck by the sombre, serious nature of her coronation. When this footage is repeated today I am mindful of the heavy responsibility placed on such young shoulders, symbolised by the large and heavy crown she wore on that great day.

Speaking of the town of Gwelo, I have omitted to say I had relatives living there, and I often visited them on Sundays. My uncle Gordon's widow Valmai Bradbury and her three children resided at 87 8th Street, Gwelo. 8th Street had seen better days, with small, unremarkable houses in quarter-acre plots. My aunt had a haberdashery shop in the town centre called Wightmans, which she had purchased from the Wightmans. The Wightmans were great family friends of the Bradburys. Valmai employed a woman who made school uniforms for all the local schools, Guinea Fowl included. Then, Miekles store, one of a chain, started selling off the peg school clothing and hand-made school uniforms are out of fashion, so ultimately, the shop failed.

'Hullo Borgie', I can still hear Valmai's sweet voice. She is a gentle person. In her youth she taught ballet, later she worked for the Department of Education. With her curly dark hair cut just beneath her ears and falling in a half circle around the back of her neck she looks very like Queen Elizabeth, the same type and style. By nature she is rather passive. She had married my mother's brother Gordon. Three children; my cousins, were born from the union. Jillian, the eldest, then Howard and Heather. When the kids are little the family lives at Lower Gwelo, about 72 miles west of Gwelo along a bad dirt road with a couple of bridges which, after the storms, cause flooding. They mine gold and it's called the Turtle Mine[37]. We rarely visit them but when we do, we make straight for the telephone which gives us access to the party line linking several families on a telephone exchange. A person wanting to call another on the exchange uses a set of distinctive rings by turning the handle attached to the phone; say three long rings and one short indicates to the person who 'owns' such rings that someone is calling. If you want the exchange you turn the handle once on a long ring. It works very well. We kids are a terrible nuisance, we use all sorts of rings to raise someone, anyone.

'Hullo, hullo, is that Jack Jones?' A multitude of giggles.

'Oh!' (Now, a posh accent). 'Mah dear leddy, I'm wanting to speak to Jack. Is he there?'

The rest of us clutch each other, pulling our clothing, hands over collective mouths, stifling idiotic giggles. The haughty voice continues, 'Well, ahm sorry, I've got the wrong number'.

We truly believe people think we are grown-ups.

There is a family called Ramsbottom on the exchange. We can't resist the Ramsbottoms – they are for it.

'Oh! Hullo'. (Very haughty!) 'I'd be so obliged if you'd tell me about your ram's bottom, and whether in fact he has a bottom'.

We cough, wheeze, gales of laughter. We are rendered so helpless, we hang up the phone. One or other of us also calls people to find out if their fridges are running. When these put-upon individuals say 'Yes the fridge is running', the retort is 'Well, you'd better run after it'.

If we're caught by one or other of our relatives, we receive a ticking-off. As for the people on the party line, they are tolerant of our silly behaviour. We also discover we can listen to other people's conversations. That's such good fun, or so we think, but in truth it is pretty boring. We soon lose interest, particularly as no-one can understand the import of what we hear. Sadly, Mum and Gordon fall out and are estranged for several years, so we don't see our cousins, Aunt or Uncle for a good while. The reason given for this estrangement is Gordon's ill-timed visit to the Hawkeys in Que Que. Mum and Dad had invited some village notaries to dinner, Gordon, for a reason unknown to me, arrives at the Residency in a filthy state. Probably he has just

---

[37] The Turtle Mine was later incorporated into the Globe and Phoenix and became known for political reasons during the 1980s. When Mugabe came to power a large number of Matabele were massacred by Mugabe's 5th Brigade, a Korean unit. Some of the bodies were disposed of down the Turtle Mine.

come from the mine and had not changed or washed. Mum is decidedly unimpressed and a blazing row breaks out. They were reconciled before Gordon dies of an enlarged heart in 1956, 'due to smoking', as our Aunt reminded us every time we spoke of Gordon. He had not turned 40.

Gordon and Valmai Bradbury, wedding c. 1937

Valmai's mother, Mrs Reese, who has dementia, lives there too.

'Hullo Mrs Reese, how are you today?'

She peers uncomprehendingly, her fine white hair escaping the bobby pins, her eyes enlarged by the thick-lensed glasses she has firmly clamped to her face. She is frail, small-boned and wears flowered dresses with a cardigan and white open-toed sandals.

'Is that you, Dolphine?' This is her standard response. Then she raves on about people and places, these phantoms from the past fill her daily life. We find it so amusing. My Aunt does not see the joke.

'Leave mother alone, you kids are the giddy limit'.

We escape into the garden where we rehash the whole conversation and giggle away.

'Hey Jillian, come and chukkaball'. She complies.

The Bradbury children, Howard and Jillian

Jillian, my oldest cousin, suffers from *petit mal*. Suddenly, in the middle of a conversation, she stops and stares blankly for about a minute. Then continues as if nothing has happened and there has been no gap in her speech. Mum tells me about this. I notice nothing unusual. She, Jillian, has a difficult life. Her father's death affects her a great deal. (Once, in 1988, when I visited her in the United Kingdom, she relates to me how desperate she felt at her father's passing.) The *petit mal* gets worse, she begins to have fits. Later, with good new drugs, the illness is effectively suppressed. She married John Knight, a young padré in the Anglican Church in Gwelo, had two still births and a cot death, but still managed to produce three lively children.

The Knights flee Rhodesia shortly after independence in 1980, during the time they live in Umtali, but that is another story.

I never get to know my third cousin Heather well. She is quite a lot younger than I, so our interests never entwine. Later, when grown-up, she lived in South Africa for some years, and is now in the United Kingdom with her husband Malcolm and children.

The author aged 18

My cousins, the Bradbury children Howard, Jillian and Heather, c. 1953

Sunday lunch with the Bradburys is always excellent. Sometimes I bring a friend from Guinea Fowl with me, but Riva told me she never accompanied me. We invariably have roast and three vegetables with lashings of gravy, followed by a large pudding. Within an hour of eating I fall asleep. The days are warm and the lunch is large. We *never* get lunch like that at school. I am sorry to say I was so involved with myself and my life at that stage that I did not think a lot about Valmai or my cousins – apart from lunch. Valmai must have been at her wit's end with money worries as her shop was not making a profit. Years later, the two older children Howard and Jillian with their respective families, moved to the UK, and she followed. Howard was particularly good to her, as she too suffered the ravages of dementia. As she tended to wander, she was in a residential home paid for by Howard and his wife Claire and she spent every weekend with them until she died. *Vale* Valmai, one of the unsung heroines that George Eliot speaks about in *Middlemarch*.

My cousin Jillian Bradbury on her marriage to Rev. John Knight

Gwelo is an unremarkable place, apart from the park and the eccentric manner in which its clock tower was built right in the middle of the main road. This was erected by a Mrs Boggie in 1937 as a memorial to her husband Maj. W J Boggie. Sometimes we walk in the Gwelo park. The park, full of flowers, manicured lawns and large shady trees, is in keeping with other public spaces during colonial times. However, the place that draws us magnetically to its portals is Marché Café on the Main Street. It had cane chairs and pale green

Mrs Boggie's clock, Gwelo

tablecloths, and they make the most delicious Knickerbocker Glories. This is a confection of fruit, ice-cream, nuts, flavouring and cream. So enormous are their Knickerbocker Glories I always feel slightly sick after consuming one. Dad quite often takes me there when he visits the school to take me out for the day. We invariably end up in the Gwelo Hotel, as is Dad's wont. He consumes his liquor and I languidly flip through the magazines in the lounge.

•

During the Rhodesian Centenary in 1953, Mum rang me one evening, 'Hullo Borgs, Tony and I are going to the Hallé Orchestra in Bulawayo and we want to take you with us'.

The fact that the Hallé visited Rhodesia at all was a miracle. Tony and she were interested in high-culture, loved opera and Tony, a man for classical music, so they decided I should be exposed to the best in world music.

'What's the Hallé?' I asked.

'A wonderful orchestra which comes from the United Kingdom and we are *so* lucky that they are touring Rhodesia, so we are taking you. We will be away for the weekend. It is all arranged'.

'But what do they do?'

(My mother's worst fears were realised).

'Play classical music'.

I discovered many of the school students were going to Bulawayo on a school excursion for the Hallé experience too.

Mum and Tony arrived at Guinea Fowl and we drove down to Bulawayo. We were to stay at the Victoria Hotel, an old-fashioned stone building, very stately. The night of our visit to the Hallé was the coldest imaginable. Southern winds blew through the city, and there is no place colder than Bulawayo when that happens. The three of us were bundled into our warmest clothes and made our way to the arena-style theatre, the Theatre Royal, which looked like a tent. In spite of appearances the Theatre Royal wasn't tented. In fact it was a huge temporary structure with a sloping floor.[38] At the time I did not know if the structure was especially built for the Hallé's visit because I did not have that sort of information. But it was a wooden edifice, raked in such a way that everyone could see the stage perfectly. The slatted seats which also served as steps were not conducive to warmth. In fact such sporting-style edifices are the worst type imaginable if the weather is inclement. The place was packed, but all of us were literally frozen, frigid fingers of cold air circulated under and through the slatted steps. I wished I had a woolen cap to wear as I could hardly feel my ears or the tip of my nose. I espied the Guinea Fowl students by their uniforms. Later Riva told me how cross everyone was at seeing the Ferrers and the two girls, Ann and Jill, in full evening dress, while the rest of them – the plebs – had to wear their school uniforms!

There on the stage were the orchestra in their black suits with white shirts and bow-ties. A man, the concert master according to Mum, was busy fiddling with his strings making a terrible racket as were others in the strings (this again according to Mum). The conductor was Sir John Barbirolli. He turned to bow at the audience, a hush fell. He stood with his arms raised, then brought the baton down. The orchestra began, with what to my mind were the dreariest

---

[38] Built for the Rhodes Centenary Exhibition of 1953 and was the biggest theatre the Federation had ever seen. Cold yes, but the acoustics were surprisingly good. (Incidentally, the Hallé also played for the Sadlers Wells Ballet who performed during the Exhibition).

sounds in the world. What did I know or care about the greats in classical music? So ignorant was I that I have no idea or memory of what concertos, symphonies or solos came forth. I fell asleep, awaking to the thunderous applause of a well-pleased audience. Mum and Tony never forgot this outing, and the fact that I slept throughout most of the performance. To their credit they were humorous about their efforts to instill culture. It was many years before I too got a liking for classical music and opera. I feel an appropriate analogy is the reading of a book like *War and Peace* when you are too young and unformed to understand or appreciate the breadth and scope of the work!

In 1955, Elvis Presley became America's heartthrob and was soon to become ours. I was living with my mother and step-father at that time, post my father's sacking from the Rhodesian Civil Service. Mum rang me at school.

'Hullo Borgs, do you want to come with Tony and me to Matapa for the Rhodes and Founders weekend?'

'Yes mummy, but can I bring Riva?'

Mum agreed.

A few days prior to our going, Gary and Robert, Riva and I discussed our plans.

'Hey, how about you get your mother to invite us to lunch on Easter Monday and we can all go home in the train together?'

The boys were planning to hitch-hike and we thought it a fine idea.

So it came to pass. We were picked up at the school by Tony and Mum. Tony was filling in for an absentee mine manager. None of us remember how long his stint lasted, but they were installed in a local house, perhaps the mine manager's home. Arriving at the mine, which was a distance south of Bulawayo about 70kms, I noticed there were at least five paw-paw trees and a bougainvillea falling over a large granite boulder. There were several blood-red poinsettias too. The countryside was rather dry and stony but the climate just perfect for growing mangos and other exotic fruits. It was a lovely Rhodesian garden of a more rugged type.

Riva and I were to share a room. We dumped all our clothing on the floor, ready to hang them up or place them in the drawers, but I doubt we ever did. Mum came in.

'Good God, Borgie, what on earth has possessed you to bring five pairs of white shoes for a three-day holiday, plus all the others?' She pointed at the muddle of footwear. 'So what are you girls going to do?'

'Play our Elvis records'. This said in unison.

She shuddered to the strains of 'Heartbreak Hotel' and 'Blue Suede Shoes'. Parents thought Elvis was the Anti-Christ because he swivelled his hips. We thought him gorgeous with his blacker-than-black hair, blue eyes, proportioned features and a voice to die for. Mum thought Elvis was the absolute pits and that we were all tainted by listening to him! However, when she was in her 80s, she professed to enjoying his music.

We were in heaven, three days of non-stop Elvis, enjoying Mum's cooking plus a bit of wandering about investigating the terrain, and hopefully, lunch with the boys!

On the Saturday I broached Mum about inviting Gary and Robert for lunch on Easter Monday.

'Fine', she said. She looked surprised. 'It's an awfully long way to come just for lunch'.

'Yes, but we can all go home together. Tony can take us all to the Bulawayo station'.

Secretly, she disapproved of my relationship with Gary – too, too much 'concentrating'. Robert's parents brought the boys on the appointed Monday. Mum made a pointed remark to Riva when Mr and Mrs Underwood left.

'What a very nice, well-mannered young man is Robert'.

Not a word about Gary. A very Mum-way of operating I thought. 'Of course', my 15 year-old mind said 'She's crazy. How could anyone not see that Gary is a very special person'.

The boys duly arrived for lunch. Mum as usual excelled herself with a slap-up dinner for us and we were all exceedingly happy and well fed. Later in the day, we were taken to the station in Tony's Rover. (In those days Rover motorcars were his favourite.) We parked outside the station and approached the platform. The whole area was filled with students from all over the country, all going back to school after the Rhodes and Founders break. We pushed our way through the crush. The noise generated by endless laughing, shouting and chattering – greetings being flung to one another, the excitement of goodbyes.

I don't remember how we knew which carriages were ours. I presume we had dedicated seats and tickets to prove this was so. We boarded the train, shouting our farewells in unison, as was every other school pupil.

'Bye-bye Mummy and Tony, thanks for the weekend'. 'Bye Mr and Mrs Bradshaw. Thanks'.

All that was left now were a crowd of spectators. The station employees looked on passively, their dark clothes and caps in sharp relief against the green-tiled walls of the platform buildings. Then with a *whoosh!* of steam, followed by a slow puffing, the engine made its stately way out of the station. We chugged past the northern suburbs of Bulawayo, the rocky outcrops fell away behind us as the country side flattened and we left the south behind. Now there was waving grass and acacia trees.

Within half an hour of the train's departure Riva and I had left our compartment to join our 'beloveds' in theirs. I am sure many other students did a big swap too. A wonderful opportunity opened up for us. We seemed to have no supervisors or teachers on that train which was packed with teenagers. It is a curiosity to this day why this was so. Perhaps they felt we were old enough to look after ourselves. This sort of freedom is not available to young adolescents today. Needless to say we had a wonderful train journey, that we both remember and talk about to this day. It was all fairly innocent. When the train finally arrived at Gwelo station and we were waiting for the school bus Riva and I laughed fit to bust.

'Fancy your mother not making the connection between the boys' arriving for lunch all that way, and the train journey back to school', she said.

Like all canny institutions the world over, the teachers decided the way to get rebellious students to conform was to co-opt them into the mainstream life of the institution. Once part of the establishment, radicals are tamed. Examples of this can be seen in many societies and authorities. Guinea Fowl was no different. Both Riva and I were made prefects in 1956. I found I was very good at bossing people about once in that role. I, who had been against all authority.

Margot Boileau our sports mistress (they were called 'mistress' in those days) took me aside. 'Remember what you were like, not even a year ago', she said. I could feel my face flame with embarrassment. I understood her perfectly.

I now had one of the individual rooms for sleeping and studying. But, strangely this part of my school years is the haziest. I put this down to the fact that having responsibility took the edge off the fun I had enjoyed in previous years. However, being a prefect introduced me more closely to boys, some of whom were older than I, and whom I had not known well prior to my elevation.

We prefects once or twice a month had formal 'Prefect Dinners' in a dining room other than our usual one, a room I had never entered until my last year at school, where we sat together for meals. I liked this. We wore our No. 1 dress, had better food, were waited on at table and of course enjoyed scintillating conversation, or at least we thought at the time it was scintillating. These dinners usually took place in the York/Lancaster Dining Hall, and I am told occasionally down at bottom school, when Mrs Goodwin was still there. I don't think the Year of 1956 went there for dinner.

Magda Siegert was the head girl and I got to know Peter Wilson, Roy Heathcote, Mike Shaw, Rory McLean and Theunis de Klerk, all prefects. Riva was also a prefect, and the year was 1956.

We also used to repair to the Prefects' Common Room for social activities. This room was a curious little wooden building on stilts. It had outside steps leading onto a small landing. There were two rooms running left and right from the landing. We met in the left-hand room. I remember we discussed politics – the Suez Canal being the topic at the time.

'Nasser will get his'. (This was Roy or Mike or Peter)

'Gyppos all of them – what a joke'.

We discussed the merits or otherwise of Anthony Eden's attempts to wrest the Suez back from Col. Nasser who had taken it unilaterally for the Egyptians. As can be expected we took the British view of things Egyptian, and were pretty racist. Later, it became obvious that Nasser was good for Egypt.

In 1956, a term before the end of the school year, our head girl Magda Siegert left school and I am told by Riva that I filled in for her until the end of the year. I do not remember this, either Riva's memory is faulty or I did not enjoy the experience too much.

During this time I heard I had a rival for Gary's affections. The girl concerned, who had let it be known to all and sundry that she had a 'pash' on Gary, was in York House. I can see her still. She was blond, blue-eyed, very pretty, a couple of years younger than I and had an older sister at school. Her name was Jennifer Hind. What to do? Frankly, I was nonplussed not being used to competition. I found it extraordinary the way in which she spoke about her feelings. I think I may have told Gary, I cannot remember, but in a very immature fashion, after all I was 16 or 17 at the time and not at all sophisticated in the ways of the world. I told everyone he was not interested in her. Bravado in every word! But it had its effect. The dark cloud quickly evaporated, my rival was probably intimidated and backed off. Our relationship continued apace. I felt very comfortable and close to Gary, and we never quarrelled. We even had a favourite song – Pat Boone's 'Moon River'. In some unconscious, no partly unconscious way, I thought we might one day get married. Such a notion had not up until that time entered my mind. Gary and I never discussed it. Mum, I realise now, was most concerned.

'You've hardly known any other young man', she said every school holiday.

'I don't care, I don't need to know anyone else'.

'Also, you are far too young to "concentrate" (with emphasis) on one boy like this. You need to get out, get away, go overseas, learn something, anything. When you've left school, that is'.

I thought she was quite mad; there would never be anyone like Gary.

One of the tasks for prefects was to arrange 'canteen' nights. Today they might call it a 'hop'. Suddenly everyone at school seemed so young and the whole magic of canteen nights diminished. I helped change records and watched while others enjoyed themselves. After the dance was finished we turned the lights out and went back to our respective hostels. Once, I remember in particular, it was decided to have a Christmas Party in Lincoln for everyone at the bottom school. I had never seen the inside of any boys' hostel and on this occasion it was the dining room that had been cleared for the party. The prefects had decorated the hall with balloons and had a turntable gramophone with all the latest hits. Boys and girls arrived, I think on the school bus.

My memory of this and all this time is rather dispiriting. There were no boys to flirt with or give my photograph to. For that is what I did in the first few years at school. Many of my colleagues had left school and it was not such an exciting place anymore. Obviously, with hindsight, I see I had been there long enough, for everything changes.

It was around this time, possibly in the last term of 1956, that a very handsome, young teacher called Mr Hart came from Cambridge University to teach English at the school. The girls thought he was just the most wonderful thing they had ever seen, with his blue eyes and dark hair. 'Heart of my Heart' was a hit that year, and we turned the words into 'Hart of my Heart' with appropriate words dedicated to him. One afternoon at the end of the school year he asked if he could take me for a drive. I was flattered. He had a little brown upright car, make unknown. Mr Hart was a highly intelligent man and talked to me about politics and the Rhodesian 'set-up' as he called it. I had never heard anyone discuss and present arguments as Mr Hart did and could. I felt far too gauche to take issue with him on anything, and, although I felt I had not given a good account of myself, that was not the last time I saw him.

As for Guinea Fowl, the year's end was approaching and I was to leave. After the usual end-of-year photos of the prefects, hockey team, cadets, rugby and cricket teams in which we all wore our best uniforms, we assembled for the last time. Our headmaster, Mr Pegg, made a stirring speech about what and who we were and how he hoped our lives would turn out. And so, it was goodbye to Guinea Fowl, the place for ever etched in my psyche!

– 11 –

Fort Victoria

After my mother and father got divorced, and in my last two years at Guinea Fowl School, Dad and John moved to Fort Victoria. He never told us anything about how or why he landed up there. John went to the Fort Victoria Public School and I spent school holidays with them. It was during these two years I returned to live with my mother and her new husband, Tony. I have no idea if Dad's move to the Magistracy in Fort Victoria was a horizontal one or just one in the natural progression of the Rhodesian Civil Service. I suspect this was a demotion for Dad, and the true facts of how this happened are not known to me.

The town is the home of the 'Zimbabwe monuments' as it is called today. We called them the 'Zimbabwe Ruins', and as the name implies we looked upon them as just that, a lot of old tottering stones, fun to visit, but worthless.

The most extraordinary thing about Fort Victoria was that it seemed an unlived-in sort of place, especially the town centre. Eerily empty it was, with extra wide streets which were so clean, it was difficult to believe humans ever stopped or walked there. A town that Australians would describe as a 'Claytons'[39] town; a town when not a town! You could throw a ball down its wide pavements and it would meet no impediment on its journey. There was a large department store, like many in Rhodesia it was called Meikles, and the usual whitewashed colonial administration buildings with a four-sided clock tower. Some sort of monument had been erected to honour the pioneer column of the BSAC led by Selous, who moved through Lobengula's Matabeleland and across the lowveld to the cooler plateau. In its early days it served as a spot from which one travelled to the mines of Mashonaland and grew into Rhodesia's largest town. When we lived there it had become rather

---

[39] A Claytons' drink is a drink which is not a drink, i.e., it has no alcohol. Claytons was a brand of non-alcoholic drink that was widely marketed in Australia in the 1970s and 1980s.

insignificant. We seldom went to town, there was nothing to do there and everything we needed was close to home.

The Residency, built in 1937 on Hay Street, was set in extensive grounds with many trees and flower-bearing shrubs. It had a tennis court, swimming pool and a fish pond under a huge tree. (As to the swimming pool, my brother reminds me of the time we had ducklings in the garden who popped into the pool and then found they could not get out as the distance between the water line and the pool edge was too high for them. We endeavoured to rescue them, they quacked their little hearts out in fear, and I like to think, in appreciation.) We had a cook-houseboy who truly must have had a difficult time. He did a mountain of work. Dad harassed him about everything he did. No gardeners this time, so the garden deteriorated markedly. I remember on my first school holiday in Fort Victoria wandering about with a head filled with how I would undertake the up-keep of the garden. I knew nothing about soil improvement, what to plant where. Neither did I know the names of any flowers or what would grow there. But I knew what freesias were and the Fort Victoria garden was filled with freesias in full bloom, they were yellow and white with some mauve, their exotic perfume almost suffocating in its intensity. So naturally, freesias are Fort Victoria for me.

The whole property had a wonderful ambience. I had a bedroom, a sort of annex/porch which had been added on to the house, with a large open area, almost the full width of the room which had wire netting instead of glass. Next to it were two or three large trees, their broad shady leaves and extensive canopy naturally reacted to the winds and rain; either soughing, gently rustling or as a background for the drip, drip, drip of rain which fell from the leaves onto the ground. I seemed to absorb it all and it shaped my instincts about climate and place.

The house had French doors leading from the main bedroom, and some from the lounge and the dining room. All these rooms faced north. At the back was the kitchen with a stable-style swing door, its brown paint slightly chipped, the bathroom, a corridor and a third bedroom, also with French doors leading on to the back garden. It, like our house in Que Que, was not made of bricks but of boards. The date of its building, 1937, was painted under the eaves on the eastern side of the house.

There were mulberry trees, many of them to the right of the fish pond. Then, at least an acre of uncultivated land. Beyond the fence was bush and an unsealed road leading to somewhere, a small hamlet perhaps.

The hospital with its bright red roof was over the road. It was surrounded by hedges and flowering hibiscus. Luckily, we never crossed its portals, and never visited a patient as we knew none. Around the tennis court grew a magnificent coral creeper, its bright pink flowers making a dramatic show. None of us played tennis, although we talked about having tennis parties which never materialised. Today, the pool and fish pond have been filled in and the tennis court turned into a mielie patch. There is no sign of the vivid coral creeper either.

Not far from us down Robertson Street, a macadamised road which became soft in the summer months, lived the Van Graans. Mr Van Graan was the local gaoler, a large man with a moustache. He was probably an Afrikaner from South Africa. He had a wife who was very much in the background of his life, she had a large stomach and unkempt dark hair. He had two daughters and a son, whom I suspect were from a previous marriage. He seldom visited Fort Victoria. The two young women, Mona and Pat van Graan, were about 21 and 19 years respectively. Mona was the glamorous one, always a perfumed picture with her slim tanned figure and light brown shoulder-length hair. Pat was plump and had a poor complexion, rather blotchy and pockmarked, but she had lovely blackish eyes. Dad fancied Mona. After all he was newly divorced, was looking after two children and had no female companion. She treated him with respect but had no interest in him. My brother who was 12 years-old at the time had a crush on Mona too.

'Quite normal, you know', opined Dad a certain tone in his voice, 'For a young boy to have a crush on an older woman'.

He repeated this often. I found the remark quite puzzling. What was he getting at?

Old Tom van Graan and Dad became great buddies. Like all civil servants in Rhodesia, the van Graans had a pleasant home and attractive garden with fruit trees at the back and a row of large spruce trees on the southern boundary. They had plenty of help with the garden. Van Graan and Dad were drinking pals. I never knew if they went to the local pub, probably not; more likely they drank at one or other of their or friends' homes.

We had an atomized existence there. The Fort Victoria public pool which we liked in preference to our own pool and sports ground were close to us too. Fêtes, dances, everything was no farther than a five-minute walk, apart from the shops which were 'in town'.

John became friendly with the Steyn family, there were several brothers, and John liked Shorty Steyn best of all. He spoke Chikarunga, the local indigenous language which John soon picked up. The pair could be seen around the neighbourhood jabbering to the locals. Shorty and John went everywhere together on their bikes. They were great friends. I remember Dad took John, Shorty and me to Tandai, I imagine for a vacation, but really don't know why we went there. We camped on the banks of the river. After erecting the sleeping tents Dad spent the whole time at the Mountain Inn Hotel which was about five miles away. We were left quite alone and the three of us entertained ourselves. The river was a beautiful spot with large rocks and pools of water set in a broad flat area. You could hear the lazy slapping of the water, especially at night.

John (second from right) and Shorty Steyn (right). Others unknown

One evening Dad was late arriving back from the pub and we had no dinner.

'What are we going to have for grub?' asked John. I scavenged around and found a packet of Chicken Noodle soup.

'This'll do. Can you fill the pot with some water, please. I'll cook this', said I.

The boys filled a large pot about two litres in capacity and boiled it on the Primus stove. Into this quantity I threw the contents of the soup packet. It boiled away. I looked into the centre.

'It's awfully thin soup, you know. Wonder what's wrong with it?' (What did I know about cooking?)

We had lots of hot water with a few noodles floating about for our supper. However, although we went hungry that night we had a carefree and happy time there. Then as suddenly as we were taken to Tandai, Dad announced one morning we were going home.

Sadly Shorty Steyn died of leukemia a few years later and we lost touch with the family.

It was in Fort Victoria that I saw *Cry the Beloved Country* based on the book by Alan Paton. The film made a great impression on me and was the start of conscious awareness of African oppression and poverty. Not to say this awakening was a moment of wanting to change things. It took me years before this truly came to the fore and in any event I was living in South Africa by then.

Occasionally we visited the Zimbabwe Ruins - a curious place, eerie, with a ruined building on the mountain top and a series of edifices on the flat. The stone walls were without render, its extent was impressive. This hill top complex of ruins, the Acropolis as it was called then, with its steep stone steps, landings and lookouts was surely a place of wonderment.[40] The hot summer air was diluted by the winds that swept over the place. The view must have been an advantage to those that dwelt there.

Archeologists regard this as a series of royal and ritual enclosures. It appears that the builders integrated whatever boulders there were into the structures as best they could. This place was inhabited for about 300 years.[41]

Down below was The Great Enclosure[42] with its sunken passageway surrounded by the thirteenth-century valley and ridge enclosures where the Rhodesian Soap Stone Bird, with its mammalian feet was found. It is the symbol of modern day Zimbabwe. The Great Enclosure, '... a royal compound and cloister for the King's mother and senior wives is the most photographed and most photogenic of all the ruins. Nearly 100m across and

---

[40] *Inharirire ya mambo*
[41] *The Lonely Planet*, January 1999.
[42] *Imba huru*

255m in circumference it is the largest ancient structure in sub-Saharan Africa'. Apparently no pre-determined plan had been formulated, it, just like Topsy, grew and grew. We knew nothing about any of this exotic history which, considering the Africans had no tradition of building in stone, and none of the stone buildings were occupied when the colonials arrived, is not peculiar. In any event, whites did not believe Africans were capable of such buildings, and the history of Great Zimbabwe seemed to have entirely faded from black consciousness. The official line was that the ruins dated from pre-Christian times. We were told that possibly the Phoenicians had built them, or the Arabs, but there was no evidence for this belief. White Rhodesians were uncurious and parochial, we knew little of history. All we were certain of was 'Blacks could not have built this, never'. I was not even aware that there was a monument to the original Fort in the town itself. In the days we lived in Fort Victoria visitors to the ruins thoughtlessly walked on the stone walls (that is the lower ones that were easy to climb) without heed for their destruction. That has changed now. If there is one place that has been looked after in post-independent Zimbabwe it is what is now called the Zimbabwe Monuments.

Zimbabwe Ruins

•

But back to the past! Dad used to tell everyone that 'When Borgs leaves school she'll stay at home and look after us'.

What a joke! I knew not how to cook, did not iron a single garment (apart from Gary's cadet kit) until I arrived in England in 1958. I liked the garden but as I have stated, had no inkling about what was required for a garden to thrive. As for budgeting, I was completely clueless about money, savings and the like. I had never known about expenses, was not aware that people had to budget, such education never surfaced in our family, so I was financially totally unschooled, all to my detriment. In any event, I wanted to get away from Dad's control and had no intention of 'looking after him'.

Dad got into fearful rages, especially during the time we lived in Fort Victoria. He never beat us, but was a past master at verbal abuse, and it was this extraordinary ability to manipulate his children that led us to stay with him when he and my mother separated. I cannot explain exactly his *modus operandi*, he had the ability to make people sorry for him. We certainly felt that way. Underneath all his bluster he was insecure and vulnerable. But we had no weapons for coping or understanding such matters. I did not realise that he was taking amphetamines, only that he was moody. One moment his disposition was merry, he would wander about cheerfully stating how he loved us and how happy he felt. Then came the black clouds, a darkness overwhelming Dad. He'd mutter about some perceived slight, complain to us about our behaviour, chivvy the cook. Who could understand it?

•

On one of my school holidays I returned to Fort Victoria from Guinea Fowl to find Dad had a new wife! She was called Margot. She tried terribly hard, poor woman. She was an ex-nurse, had acne and was facially scarred. Dark-haired, dark eyes, quite ordinary really. I knew nothing about her. She was very interested in what we ate, probably because Dad had another bout of scurvy.

'You need meat and three vegetables', she told me. 'That forms a balanced diet. Even a small amount of dessert will do you good'.

Sometimes she talked about my father. 'Ted is so unpredictable, I do not know what to do to help him'. A dolefulness overcame her at these times.

The next school holidays she had disappeared, never to be seen again. Like many a teenager wrapped up in self I never inquired as to her whereabouts – I liked her well enough but my own life was far too interesting to be bothered about Dad's sundry wives and romances. I think of Margot from time to time, she was just so much backwater in our fractured lives.

Had Dad been in his right mind, Fort Victoria would have been an ideal spot for John and me, at least while we were young. But the promise of paradise did not last. Dad lost his job. He told us he had decided to take his pension and retire, but the reality was his unbalanced behaviour due, as we now know, to his alcoholism and drug-taking had caused his downfall. The divorce from my mother added to his general malaise. In retrospect, I believe he was mentally unsound and that substance abuse helped him mask the symptoms. Today he would have been diagnosed as an obsessive-compulsive as well as an alcoholic. When you are 16, you are merely horrified, frightened and confused.

What of my brother, dear reader? Poor little chap was 12 years-old or thereabouts. He never saw his mother and in fact told everyone who inquired at that time in Fort Victoria that she was dead. On top of it he was in the custody of an out-of-control father. Dad had to give up the house and his career and, according to John, there followed a period where he was taken to every pub and snooker parlour throughout Rhodesia before the pair of them went to Sea Point in the Cape, John being sent to Christian Brothers College. Later, he too went to Guinea Fowl where he finished his schooling. After one particularly uneasy holiday Dad started talking about going on an overseas trip. I knew things were bad with Dad and no longer wanted the see-saw life at his hands. I rang up Mum.

'I want to come back and live with you and Tony. Dad is threatening to take John and me overseas. I know he has been to see the school about it, and I do not want to go'.

Mum seemed happy that at least one of her children wanted to come 'home'; she went through years of grief over John, and would have liked him back too. In reality, my mother hardly knew John after the age of 9 years, and as was illustrated much later in our lives, had no knowledge about teenagers or young people in general.

The next hurdle? How would I tell my father I would not accompany him on his crazy overseas trip? I tossed and turned, had conversations with him in my mind, going over and over what I would say, what he would say and how I would counteract that. I was frightened of Dad and his manipulative ways. I realised my resolve might fade. I had to say over and over to myself, 'No, Dad, no matter what you say, I am staying at school'. Finally I told him. He was frantic when I plucked up the courage to tell him that term-times I would be at Guinea Fowl and during the school holidays I would spend them with my mother. He arrived at the school in an agitated state, spoke to the headmaster, Mr Pegg, (by this time the Ferrers had left), to Mrs Nixon and told them all we were going to Britain. The school staff played it cool, they realised Dad had to be humoured. Then he started on me – 'sweet talking' I believe it is called. I resisted him. I put into train my mantra, 'No Dad, no matter what you say I am staying at school'. And variations of the theme. So, I set myself free, and Dad never forgave me. He and John left for their overseas trip. In Cape Town he was removed from the ship, no doubt he had behaved badly, probably boozing and taking amphetamines and dealing aggressively with passengers and crew. That's the last I saw or heard from my father and brother for several years.

Epilogue

Que Que Again, 1956

It was in 1956 that I returned to Que Que. By this time Mum and Tony lived in Central Avenue in a two-bedroomed bungalow in one of the new suburbs. It was a small ranch-style house, sunny and modern. She and I had never got on well and my return fed the old tensions, even though I was still at boarding school. Also, I felt strange to think Tony was now my step-father. Though truth is, he was good to me and put up with a lot. Mum was thoroughly irritated because I slept late in the mornings, sometimes not rising until 11am or 12 noon, so typical of teenagers everywhere. She'd complain bitterly and I felt resentful and answered her back; then we were at it hammer-and-tongs.

I remember washing my undies and hanging them in the bathroom. Her reaction was always, 'Borgie, will you please hang your underwear on the line'.

'No, I don't want to'.

'Why?' (Irritation in her voice.)

'I don't want the neighbours to see my bras'.

She got furious. She grabbed them from the towel rail, and flung more than hung them on the line. She had no understanding or patience with my reticence. On the positive side, I could decorate my bedroom with pictures of James Dean and the beautiful Rock Hudson, Pat Boone and other celebrities. She didn't mind that. I bought and played my music, like *The Student Prince*: 'Golden Days', 'Drink, Drink, Drink' – the liquid, honeyed voice of Mario Lanza who was a favourite of mine. Gary and I had been to see the film during one of the holidays. That was the year for Pat Boone's 'Love Letters in the Sand' and Debbie Reynolds in *Tammy and the Bachelor*. Life, as depicted by Hollywood, was waiting to unfold for us. I visited my friends. One of them was Lindy Jones, a very dear person, who lived with her elderly mother on the outskirts of the town. I also hung around with Jean Bradley and Eileen Sloman. We went on picnics with the local boys to Dutchman's Pool and the

Sebakwe Dam, a large slash out of the earth, with rock heaped into a jagged mountain, so typically Rhodesian, with its sandy slow-moving rocky river, its enveloping trees. We had to walk a fair way to the dam from the picnic spot, a solidly built bridge overlooking the spillway. The sun always shone at Sebakwe and the dappled and dancing lights on the water were entrancing. When I was young and the family visited Sebakwe for picnics, I used to believe they were diamonds that were waiting for me because I was a princess living in the wrong home!

•

Everything changed when my step-father got a job in Johannesburg and he and Mum left Rhodesia for South Africa. They got a thatched cottage with an established well-wooded garden down a cul-de-sac in Inanda, Johannesburg. The cottage was in the grounds of the home of a wealthy Johannesburg couple called Gundlefinger, who had several small, spoilt, sickly dogs. Mum engaged a servant called Fortunis. My memory of Fortunis was his bald head, and his being on all fours polishing the granolithic floors. One day he said to Mum, 'Madam, I am sick'.

'What's the matter?' she asked.

He pointed to the granolithic floor.

'My feet, they are crying'.

There were his footprints that, due to the heat, were sweating on the floor. We all laughed and Mum talked about that incident for years.

•

During this time, Mum and Tony agreed to look after Aunt Romola's twin boys. Her first husband had died and these were the offspring of her second husband, 'Doc' McWilliams, a tall, elegant and gentlemanly person. He owned a raincoat factory in Port Elizabeth. (She already had an older son Andrew Fyvie, whose father, a chemist, was her deceased husband). Apparently, Romola and 'Doc' were going somewhere and needed a responsible person to look after the twins. Well, they were holy terrors, but the most beautiful and angelic little characters. One was Christopher, and the other Adrian. Mum rushed around in agony, not knowing exactly what to do with them and she had to watch them constantly. She was rather fraught and anxious while they were with us.

One afternoon she dressed the twins in their little navy shorts, with braces, blue shirts and navy shoes. Their hair was slicked back and their faces washed;

we were all going to the Johannesburg zoo. About half an hour before we were to leave, Mum suddenly said, 'Where are the twins?'

We all started looking for them, calling from room to room and all around the garden. Then silently, their innocent faces appeared from the coal shed. Black they were from head to toe! I can tell you Mum was very angry and did not enjoy having to bath them and change them all over again. I did not see the twins for years afterwards as they lived in Port Elizabeth as did their half-brother Andrew.

Aunt Romola and the twins, Christopher and Adrian c. 1957

Mum was by that time sick of my loafing around the house and she asked me what I wanted to do.

'I want to be a hairdresser'.

'Terrible choice', she said, 'A job for the working class'.

'OK then I want to be a dress designer'.

They were perplexed, as I had shown no interest in dress designing.

Mum and Tony's Wedding Day with friends, 1953

Meanwhile, I felt buried in a backwater and was dreadfully homesick, I was a small fish in a large, large bowl. There was no public transport where we lived and I had no friends. I drove Pat and Tony mad playing my records. 'Great Balls of Fire' by Jerry Lee Lewis was my favourite, which I played over and over again while sitting on the veranda of the cottage. Mum's cousins, the Nicholls, Uncle Fred and Auntie Pat, came to call, and introduced me to a young fellow, but I did not take to him. We saw the Nicholls quite a bit at that stage and then, of course, later when I returned to Johannesburg to marry Peter Sherwell.

One day I said, 'Gary wants to come and visit'.

'You likea da ice-cream?' Tony's repartee.

'Well, dear, you can invite him to stay if you like', said Mother.

Gary arrived. How wonderful, how I believed I adored him and he me. I do not remember much of the visit but know it was the one really happy time I spent in Johannesburg. He stayed about a week and returned to Salisbury.

One day, completely out of the blue, John and Dad arrived in a large car for a visit. John informed me he was going away with Dad to live in the Cape, at Sea Point. When Dad and John left I remember crying my eyes out, but like many young people I found my feelings too painful and put him and my father out of my mind. In time I built an impenetrable wall against both of them. Today I realise I was in a state of grief for a long time, and it took about thirty years before I can say John and I became friends again.

One morning, after about a month of my mooning around the house, opening the fridge, eating whatever there was therein, Mum booked me into the Rosebank Commercial College (RSC) to learn shorthand and typing. At the time I was furious, but found the skills very useful throughout my life.

Every morning Tony would patiently wait for me in his Rover, for I was always late, then he would hoot. I got mad, Tony got mad and the day began badly. He would drive me to Rosebank. The College, was situated upstairs and close to what became Stuttafords in Jan Smuts Avenue. RSC was run by two Jewish women, one dark and slim with a thin, intelligent face; the other plump with red hair and lots of gold bracelets. The students clattered up narrow wooden stairs to the typing room which was about the size of an average classroom. Filled with ancient black typewriters, all of them had the faces of the keys covered. We were each given a card which showed the letters of the alphabet and how they appeared on the keyboard. We had to practice 'a,s,d,f,g' on the left-hand and ':,;.l.k.j,h', with the right hand. Later we tackled the upper and lower keys. This we did over and over again. Our efforts were marked by the teachers and we had many tests. I never did too well.

There were about twenty girls in the class, no boys. Some of these students were obviously from wealthy families. They had gorgeous black full-length coats, expensive leather shoes and bags; their hair immaculately coiffed. Shiny black sedans with African chauffeurs would glide up to pick them up at lunch-time. They never caught the bus. Mum had remarked on how raggy my eyebrows were, well, these people had eyebrows plucked with all the under hair removed, and then pencilled. It was very 'Joburg' of the '50s and '60s. I felt the ugly duckling, as I had no decent clothes, those that I had had at school were completely inadequate. I could not relate to any of the girls at the RSC. Also, I was unhappy and ate a lot and put on weight. Mother was concerned, quite rightly, and she suggested when I finished the course that if I could not settle in Johannesburg I should return to Rhodesia. First I had to get through the course. I was hopeless at typing. I did better at shorthand. I can still hear the plump tutor intoning 'Enn, downward stroke, sway hook, or Enn, e.s.t, downward curve'. We had endless lessons and assessments. I learnt all the early bits of shorthand very well but got bored with the endless contractions so did not master it as well as I might have. However, I passed in the end, got my certificate, surprisingly for both typing and shorthand, and went back to Rhodesia, vowing never to return to Joburg. But never is a long time!

I got my first job in Bulawayo, that place of the dreaded convent. Returning there was a way of slaying the dragons. I moved into the YWCA, and here again started to meet young men! My job was with a company called A. E. Davis, Chemical Importers. The boss, a Mr Davis, was a good-looking, rather quiet person who came from Durban.

Maureen Perkins was the senior in the office. 'Mr Davis' wife does not like Bulawayo, she says it is dull and dead-end and wants to return to South Africa', she told me. Shortly after she told me about Mrs Davis, I saw her, a pretty, dark haired woman who looked decidedly miserable.

Maureen was an English girl. I remember her well, she had long dark hair she wore in a bun, although she was a young woman. She had the longest legs and wore high heels which showed them off, and quite a lot of girth. Laughter and fun, that is what she represented. She went around with a young man who had a yellow car, who she always said was a friend, nothing more, and scoffed if we asked her if she was serious about him. 'Of course not'. Her eyes danced merrily. 'Anyway let's not talk about him, how about you come to the Bulawayo Club with us?' (Later she married this very same man and moved to the Caribbean).

Off we would go and spend an interesting Saturday laughing and drinking. Lots of young people joined us. The Club was a pleasant, cool place with the most gorgeous gardens and lawns. This too was so typical of colonial life. A bevy of Africans mowed, dug holes, planted trees, weeded, planted the bedding flowers, all supervised by a white, and the results were spectacular.

As you can see, social life was far more interesting than the boring work that I did, very badly, for Mr Davis. How he put up with me I don't know, but he did. Of course the money was wonderful and I soon found myself in debt at Truworths dress shop, because I could not resist buying clothes on my Truworths card. At that age I was besotted with clothing, as most young girls are, and as I said earlier I had not a clue about budgeting. Gita Westlarsen – she with the beautiful blonde hair, and the long and perfectly shaped body – was my friend. She was much sought-after, but was not easily taken in by the rakes in Bulawayo who flocked around her. Although she and I got on very well, the same could not be said for those who ran the YWCA. I was regarded as a rebel. This was because I had a great many anxiety attacks there. When the attacks passed I was so relieved I wanted to dance on the ceiling and this translated into exuberant, bad behaviour. I once spoke about the feelings of mind-out-of-body to a manageress. She said, 'You have been taken over by the devil and we should pray that you be exorcised'. Hell! That was frightening!

Although I was still technically 'hitched' to Gary, I had an infatuation for an Afrikaans man who came from Northern Rhodesia, I don't remember his name, but he was tall and lanky. The romance was short-lived as he returned to his home from which he wrote me a long, loving letter saying he would never forget me. He ended this letter with an Afrikaans simile 'Hou die blinkand bou'.[43] I never got another!

Northern Rhodesia was a pool from which many young women came to live at the YWCA. They favoured dangly earrings, lots of lipstick, gold and silver sandals and matching belts. Tanned and confident, they were quite different from most of us.

Dad visited me too. He would zoom up in his latest sports car, he crashed several of them! These were embarrassing times, he was clearly unbalanced as I mentioned earlier in this memoir.

Then he started asking my friends to go out with him. He especially liked Gita, which is not surprising, as she was gorgeous. Gita was disgusted.

'Your father asked me out'. The horror was etched in her face. I felt terrible, a burning sensation, what could I say?

•

Gary and I were still in touch with each other. I once took a train to Salisbury to spend a few days with him and his much-married mother. A very attractive woman, she was on her fourth husband then. It was a companionable sort of relationship by then, I couldn't imagine my life without Gary.

When I returned to Bulawayo, I met and went out with other young men including Mr Hart. (Strangely, I do not remember his given name). All of the faces and names of the other young men I knew in Bulawayo have faded with time. It was bound to happen, Gary and I parted, although it was never stated, we just drifted away from one another.

After I had been in Bulawayo about 18 months, Mum and Tony contacted me, telling me they were going to live in the UK. Would I like to come too? I

---

[43] A saying rather like 'keep a stiff upper lip.'

said I would go for three months – only three! I fully believed all English women wore their hair in nets and talked over their garden walls to their neighbours, similarly clad, with fags hanging from their lips. I got all this from the Andy Capp comics in the newspapers. They ridiculed me and this is an example of why they both felt that I needed my mind broadening, and that living in Rhodesia was really intellectually and culturally limiting.

They left, and I was to follow later via the Union Castle Line from Cape Town. I visited my Aunt Romola in Port Elizabeth who was going to take me to the dockside after a short holiday with her. We did a lot of shopping for clothing. It was at that time I got to know Andrew a little better. He was incredibly handsome, but was going through a 'mooning' stage. Aunt Romola told me he was constantly falling in and out of love, all of these romances 'ended in tears' she said. She could not understand why he didn't get on with his studies and forget about girls.

•

So, via the South African dockside, I said a bitter-sweet goodbye to the country of my birth. When I left on the Union Castle line, I did not, and could not foresee the future for Rhodesia, a beautiful and interesting place, but never really ours! No mind, overseas everyone was singing 'Volare' and I was taken with Dean Martin's incredible looks and his utter cool! I was going to where something big and interesting was surely awaiting me. I lived in the UK for two years, but that is another story, dear reader; however, I never once saw an English woman with a doek on her head, a fag in her fingers nattering over the garden wall to her neighbours!

ACKNOWLEDGEMENTS

Thank you to Krystal Miu Yee, Patsy Asch and Ian Johnstone of Armidale for their suggestions, reading, editing and on-going support. Also, to my children Dean and Belinda and their partners who read my MS and made constructive comments. Paul and Neil my publishers deserve a special mention for their input and interest. I'm grateful to my cousins Jillian Knight and Howard Bradbury from the United Kingdom for the photographs and anecdotes about the family they sent me and the thoughtful discussions over the years. Thanks to my cousin Andrew Fyvie from South Africa who also sent me lots of photos of the Rhodesian and South African families. Finally, Rodney Kennedy, your suggested title for this memoir was inspired, a million thanks.

ALSO FROM *Fastnet Books*

TAPESTRY OF LIFE

Short Stories by

ALF RATTIGAN

Enraged bulls in a shed full of bananas, near collisions at sea, whisky-soaked roses on coffins, weapons discharged on Sydney trams, tenacious trouser presses, trade conferences and searches for sewing machine parts – these and many more incidents, the places they occur and characters that are involved in them are all threads in Rattigan's rich tapestry of life. His stories provide glimpses into Australian social history. Not the history of momentous events, great persons (although their author was one) and cultural shifts, but the history that can be found in the odd, the eccentric and the unexpected amidst the on-going demands of the everyday. The voices found in these stories are not only that of the author but also those of people he met, sometimes only once, people he worked with and, occasionally, people he lived with. They are all Australian voices.

Fastnet Books

www.fastnetbooks.net

Also from *Fastnet Books*

A DOCKLANDS WENDIGO
CLARKE BUVELOT

A comic-horror story of the aftermath of a cover-up in the London Blitz and the investigation of the resulting presence of a cannibalistic monster in the Underground, carried out by the unlikely pairing of a veteran policewoman and a young historian, against a background of the development of London's Docklands in the 1980s.

Misadventures in London
by Paddy Jacaranda

The story of the misadventures of a young Australian during the late seventies and early eighties, mainly in London. The naïve young man sets out with vaguely politically intentions on a 'working holiday' but spirals down through alcohol and drug abuse into criminality. *Misadventures in London* recounts unique experiences and observations that reflect the place and the era.

POWERHOUSE
Angonetta Massey

When Anaeus, the sexiest guy on campus, kisses Ami, there were two things she doesn't know. Anaeus is a vampire and she has to share his affections with her best friend, Muzz, the boy next door. And there is something else, something much more important Ami needs to know —her missing father is not dead, he is undead. He is the *Karkanxholl*, the vampire zombie-master. And now he is seeking his daughter. When the killings start, Ami is driven to confront the ancient evil that lurks in the **Powerhouse**.

Fastnet Books
www.fastnetbooks.net

Printed in Great Britain
by Amazon